OUTSIDE
THE
GATE

OUTSIDE THE GATE

A Study of the Letter to the Hebrews

ROY I. SANO

Abingdon Press
Nashville

OUTSIDE THE GATE:
A STUDY OF THE LETTER TO THE HEBREWS
by Roy I. Sano

Original edition published by United Methodist Women (formerly known as the Women's Division of the General Board of Global Ministries of The United Methodist Church), copyright © 1982 by Roy I. Sano
Revised edition, copyright © 2014 by Abingdon Press

Scripture quotations, unless otherwise noted, are from the New Revised Standard Version of the Bible, copyright 1989, Division of Christian Education of the National Council of the Churches of Christ in the United States of America. Used by permission. All rights reserved.

Scripture quotations marked RSV are from the Revised Standard Version of the Bible, copyright 1952 [2nd edition, 1971] by the Division of Christian Education of the National Council of the Churches of Christ in the United States of America. Used by permission. All rights reserved.

Scripture quotations marked KJV are from the King James or Authorized Version of the Bible.

Scripture quotation marked JB is from THE JERUSALEM BIBLE, copyright © 1966 by Darton, Longman & Todd, Ltd. and Doubleday, a division of Random House, Inc. Reprinted by Permission.

Scripture quotation marked REB is from the Revised English Bible © Oxford University Press and Cambridge University Press 1989.

Library of Congress Cataloging-in-Publication Data

Sano, Roy I. (Roy Isao), 1931-
  Outside the gate : a study of the Letter to the Hebrews / Roy I. Sano.
     pages cm
  Includes bibliographical references.
  ISBN 978-1-4267-7954-1 (pbk.,trade, adhesive : alk. paper) 1. Bible. Hebrews—
Criticism, interpretation, etc. I. Title.
  BS2775.2.S26 2014
  227'.87077—dc23

                                                                    2014022854

14 15 16 17 18 19 20 21 22 23 — 10 9 8 7 6 5 4 3 2 1
Manufactured in the United States of America

Preface

Immigrants are diversifying our neighborhoods. The diversity of people will only intensify because forces driving a massive global migration will persist. The driving forces include poverty and ethnic clashes, ideological rivalries and armed conflicts, and finally, the unfolding climate changes. Even if we remain where we have lived, it feels like the ground under us has moved us to a different place. Some people seem oblivious to the changes, and others live in denial. Those who notice the changes often burrow themselves in gated and guarded communities, or in familiar and homogenous congregations of "their kind of people." As the diversity heightens the tensions and deepens the conflicts, some of our neighbors are launching attacks on "those other people" who are destroying what is dear to them. Surely there are better ways to respond to new neighbors and build a better community.

The same kind of changes challenged us when I wrote an earlier version of this book in 1982 for United Methodist Women. Before that, my family experienced animosity against foreigners. Fortunately, we also experienced God's grace through caring and courageous Christians. They left their comfort zones, went "outside the gate," and bore abuse to practice hospitality toward strangers (Hebrews 13:12-13, RSV). In the deepening diversity around us today, this study draws on the Book of Hebrews in the Bible because it beckons us to build a better city whose maker is God (11:10). Finally, at its core, Hebrews invites us to look to Jesus Christ because he is the "pioneer and perfecter of our faith" for the arduous journey ahead of us (12:2).

I want to celebrate United Methodist Women, not just because of their invitation to write this study book, but even more because of the enormous contributions they continue to make in God's mission. United Methodist Women are the denomination's best informed members through their reading programs. Because they willingly read about difficult, even controversial, issues that they cannot possibly solve, they go before God in prayer. When they rise from their knees, they bear faithful witness by word and deed to address the issues they studied. When they cannot pursue their ministries directly, they send and generously support others who can. United Methodist Women is an inviting movement to spread God's justice and love in the world.

I dedicate this book to a particular portion of that vast movement of women in The United Methodist Church, namely, the women's groups in the Japanese American churches whose historic contributions deserve memorializing in more conspicuous ways than this brief reference. I am particularly grateful for the ministry of women's groups in Oxnard, Los Angeles, El Monte, Loomis, and San Jose in California, as well as in New York City, where it was my privilege to serve.

I am grateful for the editorial work of Nancy Carter and Craig Palmer in the original edition, and to Marj Pon, Linda Ray Miller, Mickey Frith, and Norma Bates for the revised edition. My spouse, Kathleen A. Thomas-Sano, has encouraged me all along.

Contents

Chapter 1

The Living Word and Community Renewal

A Personal Testimony

Five hundred people were scheduled to come to San Francisco, California, for the 1980 National Convocation of Asian American United Methodists. Three of us were asked to prepare a Bible study for the occasion. One came from Korea, another from Taiwan, and I was born in the US to immigrants from Japan. We focused on our identity as sojourners who were still seeking to establish our home in the US. We turned to the stories of the heroes of our faith in Hebrews 11. We thought we could learn from Abraham and Sarah, as well as Moses, how to establish a new home in a foreign land. We were encouraged, but disappointed and puzzled. In the end, however, we were challenged and humbled.

We were encouraged because God provided the sojourners, Abraham and Sarah, places to flourish and enabled them to live in harmony with neighbors. We were, however, disappointed to find that God did not intend sojourners to become settlers! Abraham and Sarah "confessed that they were strangers and foreigners on the earth" (Hebrews 11:13). We wondered, then, what to make of the comforting words immigrants found in Ephesians 2:19, that Gentiles were "no longer strangers and aliens." Further reflections led us to see Abraham and Sarah were strangers in relation to the places where they lived because they desired a better country (Hebrews 11:16) and that Gentiles were no longer strangers in relation to the body of Christ because Christ had "broken down the dividing wall" (Ephesians 2:14).

Moses illustrated what was involved when we desire a better country. Earlier on in Egypt, Joseph may have saved his people from famine, but a pharaoh that reigned after Joseph turned Egypt into a place of bondage. Moses failed to convince the pharaoh to lighten their burdens, so his "desire [for] a better country" (Hebrews 11:16) led him to drastic measures in the Exodus and the arduous journey of forty years to the Promised Land.

Thus, in preparing the Bible study we celebrated provision for sojourners on their journey and a home in the household of faith. We were equally challenged, however, not to become settlers who made peace with this world, but to work tirelessly by God's grace to "overcome evil with good" wherever we lived (Romans 12:21). In doing so, we "looked forward to the city that has foundations, whose architect and builder is God" (Hebrews 11:10). We were finally humbled by our forebears who "did not receive what was promised, since God had provided something better so that they would not, apart from us, be made perfect" (Hebrews 11:39-40).

As is evident, preparation for the Bible study involved a dialogue among us, as well as with the Bible. Because the preparation bound us closer to each other and rejuvenated our faith, our interactions demonstrated what Martin Buber said: "All real living is meeting."[1]

In order to facilitate comparable interactions, the heart of this study in Chapters 3–7 includes three sections. "What It Says" summarizes a portion of the Book of Hebrews, "What It Means" suggests responses to the word of God, and "Suggestions for Reflection" lists topics for discussion in the session and preparations for what follows. These suggestions are appropriate for group or individual study. A general orientation to Hebrews will be offered next in Chapter 2. This study leads us to look to

Jesus Christ. An Appendix will elaborate on the identity of Jesus that Hebrews highlights. Aids for Further Study and a Glossary provide additional assistance. Further, definitions of words marked with an asterisk appear in the Glossary.

Dialogue With God

In the Bible, we read again and again about people expressing themselves freely in response to God's word. Sarah laughed at God's promise of a child in her old age. Abraham bargained with God to spare Sodom and Gomorrah. Moses debated with God. In the Psalms, we see startling reactions to what's happening. They question God—"Why, O LORD?" (10:1), "My God, why?" (22:1)—and dared to complain to God—"How long, O LORD, how long?" (13:1; 79:5). They even prayed for the worst on their enemies (69:22-29; 109:6-15). To walk in the light as God is in the light, means we will be fully visible before God, without hiding what we are thinking, feeling, and wishing. Only by doing so will we have fellowship with each other, and experience the cleansing, transforming work of God in Jesus Christ (1 John 1:7).

When we pray to God, we move from

- praise and adoration,
- through confession and supplication,
- to thanksgiving, intercession, and trust.

To elaborate, when we see in the Bible who God is and what God says and does in what is happening in and around us, we find occasion to praise God. Further meditation on God's actions and attributes, leads us to adoration. Before this awesome God we openly confess who we actually are, including our frailties and failures, and then offer supplications for God's grace to become the person God intends. As we then see that "God is good, all the time," and that "all the time, God is good," we offer thanks and intercede for the best God intends for others. We close our prayer "in the name of Jesus Christ," because we trust in who he is and what he will do.

We cannot always classify our prayers in such clear terms. Sometimes our prayers are more akin to sighs and groans too deep for words. The apostle Paul said these are the "first fruits of the Spirit," which will become a more intelligible expression to God (Romans 8:22-26). However clear or muddied our responses to the God we encounter, this study urges participants intentionally to pause and express themselves to God personally in private and in group processes. Such responses to God, such interactions and dialogues with God, will demonstrate, "All real living is a meeting."

The Perspective of Sojourners

Finally, a word must be added concerning a particular approach in this study. We will correlate our situations with God's word. I will begin with the experiences of Asian American immigrants and see what Hebrews has to say about who God is and what God says and does in comparable circumstances. Readers will find themselves prepared to interact with the Bible in the same fashion because we have all become sojourners in our changing neighborhoods.

We as sojourners have struggled to get ahead and find a home. Some goodness has come our way. But so have unsettling times. How can we find our way beyond our quandaries? Several crucial leads to continue our journey appear in Hebrews. This small but significant book of the Bible sets before us an inviting destination, clarifies what we must leave behind, and alerts us to distractions that can lead us astray. Hebrews also urges us to look to Jesus, the pioneer and perfecter of our faith for the journey, and promises sustenance en route for the unrelenting sojourner God intends us to be.

Before we study the heart of the Book of Hebrews, we turn to a general orientation to important features of its contents.

SUGGESTIONS FOR REFLECTION

1. Open with prayer, and have participants introduce themselves.

2. Share experiences you have had with the Bible, individually, in group study, or in worship. If participants can remember a specific passage that touched them, read it aloud and ask them to describe what happened.

3. Make it a point to read through the Book of Hebrews. Mark up your Bible with question marks, note key words, and write your reactions in a journal.

4. In preparation for the next session, read Chapter 2, "The Epistle of Paul the Apostle to the Hebrews." It addresses the familiar questions that help us understand books of the Bible: Who wrote what, to whom, why, when, and from where? List or mark the contents of Hebrews that are considered in Chapter 2.

5. Close with prayer.

The Epistle of Paul the Apostle to the Hebrews

Introduction

Up through much of the twentieth century, English versions of the Bible claimed the book we are to study was "The Epistle of Paul the Apostle to the Hebrews.*" There have been questions raised about every point in that title. Is Hebrews an epistle? Did Paul* the apostle* write it? If Paul did not write it, who did? When and where? Who were the "Hebrews" to whom it was written?

Responses to these questions will uncover key features of the message in Hebrews.

Is Hebrews an Epistle?

Given the fact that much of the viewpoint we find in Hebrews represents an exposition of particular passages from the Old Testament, such as Psalms 2, 45, 97, 102, 110, and 2 Samuel 17, some have preferred calling this epistle a "midrash." A midrash is a commentary on a biblical text by a learned teacher or rabbi. The eloquence, however, sets Hebrews apart.

Some have preferred to call Hebrews a "homily"*—an address that was to be heard in public and not simply something read in private. The writer speaks of this as an "exhortation" (Hebrews 13:22). This word could also be translated as "homily."

The reason for some reluctance in calling this writing an epistle, or letter, is that nearly all the epistles we have in the New Testament begin with an identification of its author and, more often than not, mention of the readers with some greeting for them. The New Testament epistles also close with personal messages and greetings. In the case of Hebrews, we have no usual opening or prescript, although we do have the usual ending or postscript.

The question of classification should be mentioned here because of its role in identifying the author. Although the development of arguments recall a Jewish midrash, and the writing is eloquent enough to be heard and not simply read, I will retain the classification of an epistle for the purposes of this study. It was, after all, written to be read, even if it was also to be heard.

Was Paul the Author?

Not until the late fourth and early fifth centuries was this letter associated with Paul among the Western churches centered in Rome and North Africa. At the council of Hippo in A.D. 393, and the councils of Carthage in A.D. 397 and 419, Hebrews was listed with other books as authoritative and included within the New Testament canon.*

Scholars were eager to establish that an apostle wrote Hebrews, since all canonical books were to have come from the pen of an apostle. Illustrations of these dynamics are found in the church history written by Eusebius of Antioch in A.D. 325, which reports the view held by key Alexandrians in Egypt. Pantaenus, who died in A.D. 185, thought Paul wrote it but was forced to offer an artificial reason for the anonymity. He claimed Paul could not mention his authorship because though an apostle to the Gentiles (Galatians 1:16), he was writing to the Hebrews. Early in the third century, Clement of Alexandria offered another conjecture. He said Paul wrote it in the Hebrew language and had Luke translate it into Greek. The theory had problems because it was clear the writer was using the Greek version of the Old Testament to build his case. That would have been curious if the writer and the readers could handle the Hebrew Old Testament. Paul could. Clement's student Origen apparently recognized such problems. He offered a slightly different theory. He thought Luke wrote it independently, summarizing what he had learned from Paul. In the end, it is clear he was not wholly convinced by his own theory. Eusebius said: "The truth God alone knows."

What we can establish is that the book was prized by the Eastern churches in Egypt, Syria, Asia Minor, and Greece. While it did not ever bear the name of Paul, the demand for apostolic authorship for inclusion in the canon prompted various conjectures to fit the requirements. The demand prevailed eventually. From the early fifth century the title of some translations has remained, "The Epistle of Paul the Apostle to the Hebrews." In the earliest Greek manuscripts, however, the book simply bore the title, "To the Hebrews."

It now seems unlikely that Paul wrote Hebrews. Currently, there are three major candidates for its authorship: Barnabas,* Priscilla,* and Apollos.*

Barnabas?

As early as the third century, Tertullian suggested that Barnabas* wrote Hebrews. Barnabas "heard the word" from the apostles Peter and John (Acts 4:4). If he was present in those early days, the message would have been confirmed and he would have seen that God added divine testimony by signs and wonders, by miracles, and by distributing the gifts of the Holy Spirit (Hebrews 2:3-4). Also Barnabas was a Greek-speaking Cypriot Jew, who had relatives living in Jerusalem and was a Levite* by ancestry. This could explain the lengthy discussion of the priests and the sacrificial system.

Although his name was Joseph, the apostles gave him the name Barnabas, meaning "son of encouragement" or exhortation (Acts 4:36). The author of Hebrews calls it a word of encouragement or "exhortation" (Hebrews 13:22). The same word is used in Hebrews as in Acts. As a man who sold his field and gave the proceeds to the apostles, he would have had special authority in urging his readers against living like Esau who "sold his birthright for a single meal" (Acts 4:34-37; Hebrews 12:15-17). As a traveling companion of Paul in his early missionary efforts (Acts 13:1-3), he would have drawn on the same kind of teachings at many points. This would explain some of the Pauline-like passages in the book.[1]

Priscilla?

The second alternative we consider is Priscilla, or Prisca, a leading woman in the early Christian church. At the beginning of the last century, a famous church historian Adolf von Harnack offered a case for Priscilla's authorship after he had previously argued for Barnabas. Only a few scholars have adopted the position. Ruth Hoppins has offered an update in her popular but extensive statement in 1969. Several of the major considerations she offers should be noted since she states the fullest case for a woman author of a book in the Bible.

Priscilla and her husband Aquila* lived in Corinth where it is said they had come from Rome when the emperor Claudius expelled the Jews about A.D. 49-50. Aquila was a Jew who earlier resided in Pontus, along the northern shorelines of Asia Minor on the Black Sea. Priscilla's ethnic identity or previous religious affiliation is not given. We know, however, that Priscilla and Aquila, along with Paul, were tentmakers (Acts 18:2-3).

From Corinth they traveled with Paul to Ephesus (Acts 18:18-19). They instructed Apollos, a learned man from Alexandria (Acts 18:24-28). They could have been with Paul when he returned to Ephesus and faced a riot when Demetrius, a silversmith, found his trade threatened by Paul's ministry (Acts 19:23-41). When Paul referred to them in Romans 16:4 as having "risked their necks" for him, he may have been referring to that riot in Ephesus or to a trip to Rome later when he was imprisoned. In any case, Paul mentioned their extensive fame when he thanked them. Paul referred to them in 1 Corinthians 16:19 mentioning the "church in their house."

There are several textual considerations that suggest Priscilla wrote Hebrews. First, there is the curious use of the plural and singular pronouns. Sometimes, "we" or "us" is used, and in others, "I" is used. Twice in Chapter 6 and once in Chapter 13, the first person plural is used: "Even though we speak in this way" (Hebrews 6:9); "And we want each of you to show the same diligence" (6:11); and "Pray for us; we are sure that we have a clear conscience" (13:18). The writer asks in another passage, "And what more should I say?" (11:32); and says, "I urge you all the more" (13:19) and "when I see you" (13:23). Such alterations between the plural and singular of the first person pronoun make sense if a couple that worked closely together were involved and one person did the actual writing. Priscilla and Aquila would fit the first condition.

On four of the six occasions when they are mentioned in the New Testament, Priscilla's name is listed first. This has suggested to many readers that she had greater prominence in the Christian movement than Aquila. Later catacombs and churches were named after her.[2]

Apollos?

Apollos, a native of Alexandria who was taught by Priscilla and Aquila (Acts 18:24–19:10), has also been suggested as an author. An examination of the biblical records immediately explains the reasons why he would be suggested. He was a native of Alexandria. This would suggest possible influences of Philo's orientation, which some see reflected in the dual world of spiritual realities and their earthly copies. He was described as an "eloquent man" (Acts 18:24). Many say eloquence is characteristic of the writing style of Hebrews. The epistle also reflects one who is "burning" with "enthusiasm" (18:25).

In Acts 18:28, we see one who "powerfully refuted the Jews . . . , showing by the scriptures that the Messiah is Jesus." He could do this because he was "well-versed in scripture" (18:24). This is in line with the midrashic quality of Hebrews. Each of these ascriptions is so accurate of a writer of Hebrews that it might look to some as if Luke penned these few verses in Acts to tell us who wrote Hebrews. But, of course, no such explicit reference is made.[3]

While these and other candidates for authorship illuminate various aspects of the letter, none explain it thoroughly. There have been many arguments and counterarguments offered regarding the authorship of Hebrews and there is no consensus of opinion: "The truth God alone knows."

When and Where Was Hebrews Written?

As the author of Hebrews remains at best probable, so does the place of its writing, the location of the Hebrew Christians to whom it was addressed, and the date of authorship. Origins and destinations tend to go with the author proposed. This is particularly the case with Priscilla and Apollos. If the writer was Priscilla, Corinth and Rome could be places where she wrote Hebrews and Ephesus a likely destination. If Apollos wrote it, Ephesus is probably where it was written and Corinth its destination. The points of origin and destination for Barnabas are less certain.

As for the time of writing, two observations help us establish the latest possible dates. First, Clement of Rome quoted from Hebrews in A.D. 96 in his letter to the Corinthians. Thus Hebrews could not have been written after this date. Second, the writer of Hebrews writes as if the sacrificial system in Jerusalem was still operating. Since the practices continued up to the point of the destruction of the Temple in A.D. 70, the next latest date for its writing is prior to this time. From there, it is a question of which author we accept and at what point in their lives it was written—mid-sixties for Priscilla and mid-fifties for Apollos.

Who Were the Hebrews?

The Hebrews are mentioned in the Bible when Acts 6:1 says: the "Hellenists complained against the Hebrews because their widows were being neglected in the daily distribution of food." Seven persons were then set aside to take charge of a more equitable distribution.

The Hebrews were probably Jewish converts to Christianity who wanted to retain a greater adherence to the laws of Moses than was encouraged by the early apostles to the Gentiles. There were great numbers of Jewish converts to Christianity (Acts 21:20). Many of them remained "zealous for the law" and complained that Paul did not urge the Gentile converts to strictly observe the laws of Moses. They were Christians who spoke Hebrew or Aramaic (which was quite close) and retained a bias for Jewish expressions of religion. Most had Jewish ancestry; some were Gentile proselytes* converted to Judaism.

In any case, the Hebrews felt that God had been revealed in Judaism and were comfortable with these historic and familiar ways of expressing their faith in God. They resisted new and different religious expressions.

The Hebrews to whom this writing is addressed seem to have been particularly drawn to an earlier period in Israel's history— the sojourn in the wilderness. This is probably why the author dwelled on figures, symbols, rituals, and moral codes associated with the wilderness journey. He referred to angels,* Moses, Joshua, the Levitical priesthood and its key sacrificial rites, to the covenant* and the law delivered during that period, and the Tabernacle (or "tent of meeting"). The Temple was constructed later. The writer uses Mount Sinai* as a point of contrast with Mount Zion* in Jerusalem.

An interest in the wilderness sojourn was characteristic of a particular strand of Judaism that included people who had become disenchanted with the religious developments that they saw in the Jerusalem priesthood after their return from exile. Further, they felt the people had departed from the old covenant. They expected God would bring an end to this degenerated state of affairs and would reinstate a restored Judaism purified of all the errors that dominated their day. This mind-set continued a major force in their ethos for centuries.

The conditions they longed for would be inaugurated through special agents reminiscent of those they had known in the past. God acted in the angels of death and had given the law to Moses on Sinai, so they looked for a supernatural agent. And as Moses had led them out of bondage in the past, and Joshua had led them into the Promised Land, so too they could expect God would act through similar leaders who would lead them back to the Promised Land. The reigning one, a royal figure, would reign like a priest* who would put them back in touch with God through the purified rites. People would live out the will of God in a new covenant.

These people established communities in the Judean desert near the Dead Sea as a sojourn while preparing for a new city of God. For people who waited for an entry into the Promised Land, it was no wonder they would use the wilderness sojourn as the model for their life.

Such communities, or variations of them, had influences far beyond the confines of the Judean desert and could have influenced the Hebrews to whom this letter was written. For instance, the Essenes,* who shared several of the major tenets of faith and practices with the Qumran community* near the Dead Sea, are known to have had an influence in such distant places as Ephesus in Asia Minor. Also, Jews who were influenced by such communities and who were converted to Christianity could be expected to have retained some of their old religion. If they were Hebrews in temperament and believed God's actions were best expressed in Jewish forms of religious life, they would have carried these same practices and expectations into their Christian life. As Christianity moved outside its strictly Jewish expressions into the larger Gentile world of Hellenism, they were unprepared to appreciate the saving actions of God among people who had a different cultural expression of that faith.

In conclusion, we can say with greater certainty that the Letter to the Hebrews was written for Christians who wanted to express their faith in familiar Jewish forms and were less open to new modes of divine action. As for the likeliest candidates for authorship of that kind of message, we are less certain. Three are among the ones worth considering for readers of this present book: Barnabas, Priscilla, and Apollos.

WHAT IT MEANS

The Epistle to the Hebrews for the United States

We live in days that are quite similar to the transitions that characterized the time when Hebrews was written. In 1980, Walbert Bühlmann described the changes the church faces. As we come to the beginning of the third millennium of Christian history, he observed, the leadership of the church will pass into the hands of the Third World (Latin America, Africa, and Asia-Oceania). At that point, we will see a Third Church, quite distinct from the two previous churches, dominate the global scene. It will replace the Second Church, based in Europe and North America, which gave leadership to Christianity during the second millennium. The First Church was led by Eastern Orthodoxy during the first millennium. Walbert Bühlmann's prognosis has been fulfilled because of the surge of energy in the Third World. By the year A.D. 2000, Third World Christians outnumbered European and North American Christians.[4]

We are experiencing the impact of this budding reality in the United States. Ethnic minorities are growing at a more rapid rate in our population than whites. While great numbers of racial minorities belong to religious bodies outside the mainline Protestant denominations, their influences are felt in these denominations. The greatest growth potential of these denominations appears among African Americans, Hispanics, Native Americans, and Pacific and Asian Americans.

Many of the spiritual struggles that the writer of Hebrews addressed are the issues we confront. The overwhelmingly white part of The United Methodist Church, for example, will be, as a whole, intimidated by the changes. If we expose ourselves to interactions with these Third World Christians, we will find many of our favorite Bible passages challenged. New passages will take their places. Standards for Christian conversion in evangelism and mission will be altered. In the past, we may have been teary eyed about a picture of our sacrificial service for the "needy." Instead we will be told of the insult and inhumanity that permeate the gestures extended to the "down and out." These Christians will remind us how they are on the rise and on the inside. They will point out to us the first two churches are on their way down and outside the main currents of historical developments.

Just as the early Christians that had known much about God in Judaism, members of predominately white denominations, which have histories in the United States or Europe, will be tempted to withdraw into the familiar expressions of their faith. If their responses are not guided by biblical faith, nostalgia will lure them, not the call of God to move into a new era of Christian witness. Sloth will overcome many.

The reason for nostalgia and sloth will be understandable, though not excusable. United Methodists are beneficiaries of a Christianity that has flourished for centuries in North America and Europe. The understanding of God, the Savior, the church's ministry, and much more are inextricably bound up with the perspectives of European civilization.

This culture determines the music we sing, the clothing we wear, and the food we eat at the holy moments. For instance, in generous gestures and/or as an entertaining diversion, we may occasionally eat rice cakes, not bread, and drink tea, not the fruit of the vine at the Lord's Supper. But in the moments when we celebrate a birth, consecrate a marriage, or memorialize the deceased, we fall back on those familiar modes of worship.

The long history of these practices suggests they have proven their worth. Confirmations abound for us. Famous musicians play and replay our sacred music in the finest concert halls. Museums enshrine paintings that memorialize our past. Prestigious libraries guard records our forebears kept. Eminent scholars pore over our history in yet another attempt to solve a minuscule problem. People from distant places come to pay homage, emulating what we have done. All of these and much more reinforce our preferences for the way God has been encountered in music, readings, and buildings familiar to us.

The spirit of the Hebrew Christians appears in various forms in the church during times of transition. What is sobering is the grave threats it poses for the body of Christ. When the Hebrews could not accept the Hellenists—the Gentile converts with a different ethnic identity and a distinctive culture—the Hellenists were relegated to subservient status. Hellenists served tables while Hebrews played prominent roles (Acts 6:1-7). Eventually, the Gentile Christians created movements of their own, where they could live in fuller dignity. Christians centered in Rome broke away in A.D. 1054 from the Eastern church. In turn, those living beyond the Alps divorced themselves from Rome in the sixteenth century. One group even bore the name of their ancestors and called themselves Anglicans. Later, when the Anglicans could not fully appreciate the new movements of the Spirit among those who were marginalized by industrialization or were far removed by colonization, the Methodists were forced to break away.

Groups attached to familiar modes of God's action have not always been receptive to new models of God's saving efforts. People associated with the new and different movements of divine action have therefore created separate organizations and thus divided further the body of Christ. That groups will be different is not debated here. When differences introduce divisions, we must speak of it as pulling apart the body of Christ. Those who have known God through one cultural mode often drive away those who wish to give witness to the fullness of God in different forms. Efforts for reunion may proceed today, but the spiritual issue represented in hankering for the past still remains with us. We need to hear the word of God from the Epistle to the Hebrews or we face divisions in the household of faith.

Our picture of forces at work in changes we experience determines our behavior. Insightful comments by Dr. F. Thomas

Trotter, who was the General Secretary of the General Board of Higher Education and Ministry in The United Methodist Church, depict what is at stake. Drawing upon the book *The Beaches Are Moving*,[5] he illustrated the difference between seeing erosion or migration in the changing shorelines. If we see the beaches suffering erosion, he explained, we take a course of action to try to stop it. We assume the beaches are stable, when in reality they are "in a constant state of flux. . . . To 'stabilize' the beach is to add to the change, not to stop it. . . . [Erosion] 'carries with it the sense of irreparable loss of vital land, images of the Dust Bowl and gullies on worn-out southern farms. . . . Moving shorelines are trespassers to be subdued and evicted.'"

If we see shorelines migrating, he continued, we "'see no permanent loss. . . . [We see] islands rolling over themselves in tank-tread fashion. Migration, whether for birds or beaches, is the process of travel for the sake of survival.'"[6]

Imagery from Asian immigrant heritage may help depict the positive alternative in Dr. Trotter's eloquent message. We were transient workers constructing railroads, or farmhands moving with the crops. Recovering the sanctity of that heritage that once embarrassed us has helped us speak of God as the Migrant Worker. This God marshals all the elements in the environment, as "islands rolling over themselves in tank-tread fashion" reshape their shorelines. So, too, this Migrant Worker is moving into new arenas in human history and releasing redemption through unique cultures of emerging peoples. The fundamental question the Epistle to the Hebrews raises is whether Christians will follow the Migrant Worker, or will they demand this God stabilize the moving boundaries of our faith?[7]

If the Second Church receives the news of the emerging Third Church in the third millennium as an erosion of the eminence and purity of Euro-American Christianity, we will see the potential for irreparable loss and wish to stop the process. We will find ourselves treating Third World people and their counterparts in the US as trespassers who must be subdued and evicted. Instead, will Christians in the Second Church play the midwife as these Third World people uncover a heroic past they had repressed? When those stories are told of God's mighty acts through them, will we move beyond the guilt, anger, and envy that may be prompted inside us? Will we sing the hymns they compose, dance the poetry they write, cry and shout the litanies they pen? Will we encourage them when they convert downtown churches we left behind into community centers? If we do so, we will be moving with the Migrant Worker, who is still creating and redeeming.

SUGGESTIONS FOR REFLECTION

1. Share features or key points in Hebrews described in Chapter 2.

2. In "What It Means," the text claimed that the challenges of changing cultural expressions of the Christian faith in the Bible recall those we are facing today. Describe new cultural expressions of the Christian faith that you have encountered— differences in age, ethnicity, gender, and so on. Did you respond as the Hebrews did toward Gentiles? Which responses are desirable? How might our responses improve?

3. In preparation for the next session, read Hebrews 1 and 2, before and after you read Chapter 3, "A Pioneer Worth Following." Does "What It Says" describe the content of the sections? If not, how would you describe the content? In "What It Means," what are the distractions that could lead us astray on our journey?

Chapter 3

A Pioneer Worth Following:
Hebrews 1–2

Introduction

Marshall McLuhan, the communication specialist and educator, coined the expression, "the medium is the message."[1] According to him, various media—and not the content they try to communicate—shape our lives. He has argued that television in particular makes us visually dependent and less skillful in verbal assertions. We become more passive and reliant on information in quick capsules. Such impatience with careful considerations would make books obsolete. McLuhan decried the soothing impact that the media exercises. It thwarts human development.

Similar considerations begin the Epistle to the Hebrews. The text says that some media of divine communications can become so important they can distract our attention from the message. There is only one instance in which a medium of God's disclosure coincides with the message God offers. That medium is Jesus. The consequence of this medium as the message is not ominous but hopeful. Jesus is therefore the only pioneer (2:10) worth following.

What It Says

God Has Spoken in Many Ways
(Hebrews 1:1-4)

While affirming God's action through ancient Judaism, the writer of Hebrews was eager to establish that Jesus was the medium through which God had most fully communicated the divine message. In that sense, the author argued, Jesus is superior to angels, Moses, Joshua, the priests and kings, the sacrifices, the old covenant and law, and the hopes for a city on earth.

The writer's understanding of Jesus can be analyzed around three traditional roles. They appear in Hebrews 1:1-4, which we can consider as an introductory section.

> Long ago God spoke to our ancestors in many and various ways by the prophets, but in these last days he has spoken to us by a Son, whom he appointed heir of all things, through whom he also created the worlds. He is the reflection of God's glory and the exact imprint of God's very being, and he sustains all things by his powerful word. When he had made purification for sins, he sat down at the right hand of the Majesty on high, having become as much superior to angels as the name he has inherited is more excellent than theirs.

While there may be some overlap in the meaning of roles, distinctions can be drawn. Jesus is one who expresses God, purifies us of sin, and reigns with God. For students of Scripture and theology, these roles traditionally bore the titles of prophet,* priest, and king.*

The introductory section states that previous messengers had indeed communicated God's word, even if they were in partial and varied ways. But, unlike these *prophets,* Jesus spoke for God as a Son. A Son can express God's message fully and completely because he bears the very stamp or character of the Parent. Since the divine Parent creates and sustains the world, the Son is creating and sustaining the universe. We could say of this one who plays these roles that he is the word or expression of God's power and reflector of divine glory.

Because the things God created and sustained had gone awry, Jesus as a *priest* made possible the purification of sins. Jesus' work was so complete that he took a *kingly* role and reigns at God's right hand. That role will be fulfilled when he becomes heir of all things in accordance with his appointment.

The analyses of various portions of Hebrews will proceed on the assumption that these three figures of prophet, priest, and king reappear at several crucial points in the text. First one, and then another figure may be highlighted in the presentation, but the other roles or figures inevitably reappear in one image or another. Thus, the Letter to the Hebrews will be read like something comparable to a spiral. We will return again and again to the same three figures under different images.[2] Each time we go into a new round we will find further elaborations while references will point to the background and hint about what follows.

The Major Issues
(Hebrews 1:5–2:18)

The first two chapters of Hebrews compare Jesus to angels. But why angels? Can such comparisons serve any useful purpose for us today? An examination of the historical situation that the writer was addressing and a review of the arguments the writer employed will suggest the applications we can make in our day.

Our English word for *angels* is a Romanized version of the Greek word *angellos*. Although we translate the original Greek word as "angel," we can also translate it as "messenger," that is, the means or medium of communication. The writer was therefore comparing Jesus to messengers whom God had used. The question was whether the readers would be guided in their sojourn by the expressions of God through a Son or distracted by angelic bearers of God's word.

The Hebrews' attachment to angelic messengers is quite understandable, given the world of thought and symbols that ancient people used. God had communicated with people in a variety of ways. A plant, such as a burning bush, could communicate God's word to Moses (Exodus 3:2); a beast of burden, such as Balaam's ass, could utter a word for God (Numbers 22:28); and human beings, such as the prophets, could proclaim, "Thus says the LORD! . . ." (Amos 1:3). In addition, there were superhuman modes of divine communication through angels, such as Gabriel, who told Mary that she would bear a son, Jesus (Luke 1:26-31). Because there were angels who were untainted by sin and error, they had special status among the messengers of the Almighty. Particular angels, such as Michael (Revelation 12:7), were given superior status among the messengers. One could expect even more from them.

These viewpoints about messengers are reflected in the Dead Sea Scrolls, from the period and place close in time to Jesus and the original Christian community. The documents come from a people who had renounced the priesthood in Jerusalem and went into the Judean desert near the Dead Sea. They longed for the restoration of a purified priesthood, with its rituals, covenant, and laws. In accordance with Deuteronomy 18:18, they expected another Moses, who would lead them back from the wilderness where they were dwelling, just as Moses had done in the past. The inaugurator of that age was to be the archangel Michael who would upstage other servants of God, including the king and priests of that time. Recorded in these Dead Sea Scrolls are expectations that are the major issues Hebrews addresses: angels, Moses, a king, and the priesthood—along with their rituals, laws, and covenant. The comparison in Hebrews 1:5–2:18 between Jesus and angels is therefore not accidental or artificial. People looked to superhuman messengers for the divine word and action. The media upstaged the divine message they were expected to communicate, just as in our days the media can draw us away from the substantive message that they could convey.

It is not far-fetched to imagine that the religious outlook of this Judean community or of ones that shared similar views influenced

Christians in the early decades. One possibility is that converted Jewish priests (Acts 6:7) were among those who were "scattered throughout the countryside of Judea" (Acts 8:1) during the early persecution. They could have found these views in the Dead Sea Scrolls attractive and in turn influenced other Christians. Or these documents would reflect more widely held views that could have shaped Christian thought elsewhere. If these influences did occur, the consequence is what we should notice.

If angelic messengers assume this commanding position, who deserved to be heard and followed? Was it Jesus or the angels? Would it make any difference? In answer to these questions, the writer of Hebrews compared Jesus and the angels and urged readers to give heed to Jesus.

The writer's argument is the following: because angels are at best servants and "ministering spirits" (RSV), we must not confuse these media of God's communication with the message itself, even if they are superior to human beings. We must look beyond these media to God's communication, which finds its fullest expression in a Son. Only in this instance of Jesus as a Son do we have one who is at the same time the medium and the message. By looking to angelic messengers, we could find ourselves sadly misled because they cannot accomplish what the Son of God can perform.

A critical point is worth noting. The writer of this epistle might have been drawing upon an insight in the Hebrew language. The term *davar** in the Hebrew language can be translated as word and deed, message and activity, expression and event. A communication had a consequence. In Isaiah God says, "So shall my word be that goes out from my mouth; / it shall not return to me empty, / but it shall accomplish that which I purpose, / and succeed in the thing for which I sent it" (Isaiah 55:11). The Son not only expresses God but also acts out the divine intentions. Not only is the medium/messenger and message one, but the communication accomplishes the intentions. The Son combines both meanings: resemblance that is expressive of God and implementation of God's reign.

The situation has been sketched and the first round of the midrash has been outlined. It should now be easier to analyze in greater detail the contents of the next section appearing in Hebrews 1:5–2:18.

Jesus Is Superior to the Angels
(Hebrews 1:5-14)

Since the audience took God's utterances seriously, the writer claimed that none other than God had called Jesus a Son. As God addressed one as a son in Psalm 2:7 and promised that one would continue as son, so God addressed Jesus. In addition, angels were to worship the Son because they are servants (Hebrews 1:6-7, 14). The reason is that the Son reigns unerringly with righteousness and undergirds the cosmos unfailingly (1:5-14).[3]

> For to which of the angels did God ever say,
> > "You are my Son,
> > > today I have begotten you"?
> Or again,
> > "I will be his Father,
> > > and he will be my Son"?
> And again, when he brings the firstborn into the world, he says,
> > "Let all God's angels worship him."
> Of the angels he says,
> > "He makes his angels winds,
> > > and his servants flames of fire."
> But of the Son he says,
> > "Your Throne, O God is forever and ever,
> > > and the righteous scepter is the scepter of your kingdom.
> > You have loved righteousness and hated wickedness;
> > > therefore God, your God, has anointed you
> > > with the oil of gladness beyond your companions."
> And,
> > "In the beginning, Lord, you founded the earth,
> > > and the heavens are the work of your hands;
> > they will perish, but you remain;
> > they will all wear out like clothing;

like a cloak you will roll them up,
and like clothing they will be changed.
But you are the same,
and your years will never end."
But to which of the angels has he ever said,
"Sit at my right hand,
until I make your enemies a footstool for your feet"?
Are not all angels spirits in the divine service, sent to serve
for the sake of those who are to inherit salvation?

(Hebrews 1:5-14)

Heed the Words of the Son
(Hebrews 2:1-4)

If angels are to worship the Son, people are called to give heed to the Son. The phrase "pay greater attention" indicates focusing on Jesus' lead to listening and obeying God. Just as the Hebrew term *davar* means word and action, so the term *shama** means listening and obeying, hearing and acting in accord with what is heard. To "heed" is to hear and obey.

> Therefore we must pay greater attention to what we have heard, so that we do not drift away from it. For if the message declared through angels was valid, and every transgression or disobedience received a just penalty, how can we escape if we neglect so great a salvation? It was declared at first through the Lord, and it was attested to us by those who heard him, while God added his testimony by signs and wonders and various miracles, and by gifts of the Holy Spirit, distributed according to his will. (Hebrews 2:1-4)[4]

A warning is issued against drifting away from the message and disobeying or transgressing it. If the message delivered by angels (Galatians 3:19 and Acts 7:53) brought adverse consequences (Exodus 32:33, 35), so too will disregarding Jesus who is the Word of God. (See also Hebrews 10:29-31.) This message was expressed directly from the Lord and had consequences that lent support to the greatness of the salvation that was proclaimed (2:3-4). Externally, signs, wonders, and powerful deeds accompanied the proclamation in Jesus (Acts 2:22) and in the early church's work (2:43). Internally, the presence of the Holy Spirit made conspicuous changes in character (Galatians 5:22-23). Thus, the one we are called to heed offers a truly great salvation that must not be disregarded. This salvation transforms people, endowing them with abilities to do mighty deeds.

Following these references to the greatness of the salvation offered by Christ, the author elaborates on the kingly qualities in Jesus. God has not subjected the world to angels; God has put everything under subjection to the "Son of Man.*" The phrase, "Son of Man," in this context refers to the one who reigns and hence has kingly qualities (Hebrews 2:6-8, from Psalm 8:1).[5]

> Now God did not subject the coming world, about which we are speaking, to angels. But someone has testified somewhere,
>
> > "What are human beings that you are mindful of them,
> > > or mortals, that you care for them?
> > You have made them for a little while lower than the angels;
> > > you have crowned them with glory and honor,
> > > subjecting all things under their feet."
>
> Now in subjecting all things to them, God left nothing outside their control. As it is, we do not yet see everything in subjection to them. (Hebrews 2:5-8)

Dangers of Drifting Away (Hebrews 2:5-8)

The writer of Hebrews confronted a spiritual battle. Certain ones among the faithful were drifting away from Jesus, who was central for their salvation. They were not following "the pioneer of their salvation" (2:10). Some persons were drawn toward superhuman modes of God's communications and expected these messengers to achieve more than they could. These persons forgot the distinction between the medium and the message. Angels were only a means of communication, not the content of the message itself. Only Jesus was a mode of divine expression that could also execute the divine intentions because he was a Son, and as Son was a reflection and the very stamp of God. The salvation this God offered transformed people and endowed them with gifts for a mighty work. Those who pass up this grand gift will find in God's judgment an awesome fate. But this God of justice was also merciful and compassionate. People could find in this Jesus one who could help in time of need.

By comparison then, Jesus was superior to angels as an embodiment of God and not simply as a communicator of words and messages. While this placed Jesus far above angels as one who reigns, Jesus was also below the angels in the sense that he lived in our world of temptation, suffering, and death while offering a saving presence.

Jesus Is Close to Us
(Hebrews 2:9-18)

If the one who reigns was on the whole elevated far above the angels and hence removed that much farther from us, Jesus as a priest is also close to us.

> But we do see Jesus, who for a little while was made lower than the angels, now crowned with glory and honor because of the suffering of death, so that by the grace of God he might taste death for everyone.
>
> It was fitting that God, for whom and through whom all things exist, in bringing many children to glory, should make the pioneer of their salvation perfect through sufferings. For the one who sanctifies and those who are sanctified all have one Father. For this reason Jesus is not ashamed to call them brothers and sisters, saying,
>
> "I will proclaim your name to my brothers and sisters,
>> in the midst of the congregation I will praise you."
>
> And again,
>
> "I will put my trust in him."
>
> And again,
>
> "Here am I, and the children whom God has given me."
>
> Since, therefore, the children share flesh and blood, he himself likewise shared the same things, so that through death

> he might destroy the one who has the power of death, that is, the devil, and free those who all their lives were held in slavery by the fear of death. For it is clear that he did not come to help angels, but the descendants of Abraham. Therefore he had to become like his brothers and sisters in every respect, so that he might be a merciful and faithful high priest in the service of God, to make a sacrifice of atonement for the sins of the people. Because he himself was tested by what he suffered, he is able to help those who are being tested. (Hebrews 2:9-18)

An analysis of this rich section asserts that Jesus became a "merciful . . . high priest in the service of God." A priest is one who goes before God and brings God's goodness to the people. To do so, as a high priest, Jesus took on our nature of flesh and blood. In that life, Jesus was tempted, suffered, and died. Through his death, however, Jesus destroyed the one who had the power of death, namely, the devil, and delivered all those who through fear of death were subject to a lifelong bondage. Jesus thus became the pioneer and author of our salvation.

What It Means

Dangers of Distraction En Route

The writer of Hebrews has encouraged readers to follow the pioneer of our salvation (2:10) and warned against drifting away when we are distracted by something else (2:1). In Hebrews 12:1, the author further urges readers to set aside "every weight and sin that clings so closely" so that we can run freely the race set before us. The church's fellowship, worship, organizations, and Bible can become weights. Unlike sins that are evil, weights are good things that can hamper our pilgrimage.

We need to be clear about the difference between the media of God's message, such as angels, the Bible, and key religious figures, which are good, and the message itself. There is only one instance where the medium or messenger (Jesus) and the message (salvation) coincide. In all other instances, the writer of

Hebrews urges that we distinguish between the medium and the message. No matter how superior these media are to us, we are reminded that they are subordinate to the pioneer of our faith whom we are called to follow.

Since the Bible can play that distracting role for Protestants, it will be appropriate for us to reflect on applying the writer's concern in this section (1:1–2:18) to our salvation. To begin with, we should be very clear about one point. This spiritual growth study intends to heighten the effective use of the Bible among churchgoers. For far too many of our people, the Bible is a closed book. It remains off-limits because it intimidates people. Under the circumstances, these people can turn the Bible into a charm. They keep it close by in case of emergencies. It sits on bookshelves at home or gives comfort when a Gideon Bible is found in a hotel. This spiritual growth study will hopefully open a closed book, nudge the timid into the off-limits, and turn the charms into a companion for our sojourn.

For others, the Bible has become a fetish. They may have found the Bible particularly helpful in a crisis. What happens to individuals is reflected in Protestant churches. A fuller analysis of these dynamics therefore can help us understand what is happening and thus prepare us for a full practice of the actions the writer of Hebrews encourages.

We are spiritual heirs of the Reformation, which recovered the constructive place the Bible can have for our lives. Whereas, on the one hand, one might say that for medieval Christians "the church created the Bible"; on the other hand, "the Bible created the church" for Protestants of the Reformation. As with other slogans, this formulation has its limitations; however, it also has value.

The medieval church saw how dependent the Gospel records were upon the early church. Out of the faith and struggles of the church, certain writers gave witness to Christ. Later, the church, guided by the Holy Spirit, determined which ones of the books belonged in the Bible and which should be left out of the canon. The church played a crucial role in producing the Bible in at least these two senses. Hence, the Bible belonged to the church to copy, translate, and interpret—particularly through certain designated leaders who were charged with that responsibility. This, of course, came to mean the clergy and not the laity.

While these developments were all very understandable, the abuses became extensive. As a corrective, the Reformation therefore claimed the Bible belonged to the people. Through the guidance of the Holy Spirit and the help of others, people could hear the word of God. The church did not sit in judgment on the Bible, but the Bible could judge the church and correct it. Those who read the Bible with an open and trusting heart could meet the living Christ. They could become Christians and thus join the church. In this way the Bible creates the church. Eventually, with Protestants having such a profound appreciation of the Bible, it is understandable the Bible would become so prominent.

Only a few steps remain before the Bible becomes an idol. We begin to protect it and claim more than we can for it. We make it superhuman by claiming that it is without error, just as the ancients found themselves elevating certain messengers because they were thought to be without sin or error. A great variety of efforts have been undertaken. Arguments were devised to establish the accuracy of the Bible to the last detail. As we read some of the intellectual gyrations offered to prove the inerrancy of the Bible, we can understand why some people have turned to superhuman angels.

God has used all kinds of media for communication, such as plants and animals, and even inadequate and sinful Peter as a messenger. We therefore should be open to God using a Bible that contains historical inaccuracies, some outdated standards, and utterances of God applicable to very specific situations and cannot be generalized. Some persons who want a superhuman media of divine communications will resist such admissions. The trap of idolatry waits for them. They will find themselves trusting the Bible more than God intended.

From the late nineteenth and early twentieth centuries, Protestant churches in the US have been split over the status of the Bible. Clergy and laity have been run out of local churches because they acknowledge that the Bible contains errors and could be misleading when a particular command is overextended beyond its historical usefulness. No, the ancients' desire for a superhuman medium of communication has not been left behind. People still want some creaturely medium to become something as perfect as only God can be, or the very stamp of God only found in the Son of God.

This spiritual growth study is an effort to take the Bible seriously, even if it is not taken literally at every point. While this study may offer a critique of the approaches that make the Bible into an idol, it also offers a way of making the Bible a means of receiving the message through it. As the hymn has it, "beyond the sacred page I seek thee, Lord."[6] Jesus is the one we must listen to, he is the one who is the Son, and as Son, he reigns with power and yet is our companion who lives with us amidst our temptations, sufferings, and death. Anything else, no matter how good it may be, can distract us from following Jesus in the sojourn that the writer of Hebrews urges us to pursue.

SUGGESTIONS FOR REFLECTION

1. Review the attitudes the ancients had toward angels or messengers. Once the attitude described in this study seems to be grasped, evaluate the modern parallels drawn in "What It Means." Is it a fair analogy to draw? How do you feel about the authority of the Bible? Does authority rest on historical accuracies, such as including the various lists of kings in the Old Testament histories and the numbers of people present at a miracle, or the sequence of events after the resurrection of Jesus? Can you believe God uses a frail medium of communication, even if such frailty is discovered in the Bible?

2. How do you feel about the goal of building a faith community through this spiritual growth study?

3. Spend some time in small groups or in silence considering the outline of prayer in Chapter 1 (page 3). Consider, if any, responses to the discussion, for example, concerning our attitudes toward

the message (pp. 21–30 and Appendix) and other messengers. Are there adorations, or confessions, or any other response?

4. Prepare for the next chapter. If this resource is used in a study group, assign persons to summarize their evaluation of the section in the next chapter concerning the "destination" as a "household," "rest," Moses and Joshua, or the high priest. Read the relevant biblical passages as well as react candidly to the analysis. Watch for the role of Christ as the model for our action that is implied or mentioned.

Chapter 4

Pressing Toward Distant Destinations:
Hebrews 3:1–5:10

Introduction

Trek Through the Wilderness

This chapter studies Hebrews 3:1–5:10, the next, 5:11–6:20. They are held together by a basic metaphor of ancient Israel's trek through the wilderness. Thus, when the writer of Hebrews tells the reader who Jesus is, he (or she) compares Jesus to Moses and Joshua, two central figures during that period of Israel's history. Further, when he tells Christians where they are headed, what they are asked to leave behind, and what is required en route, the writer uses illustrations from the forty-year journey of the children of Israel.

Because most of what we read in Hebrews 3:1–6:20 emerges out of the root metaphor of ancient Israel's pilgrimage through the wilderness, this chapter and the next one will be seen as a unit. Considerations in this chapter will be gathered around the destination the author depicts and in Chapter 5 will be clustered around the point of departure. Chapter 3 dealt with distractions from the pioneer who leads the pilgrim people of God.

A Heavenly Call

Hebrews 3:1–5:10 begins with the following words:

> Therefore, brothers and sisters, holy partners in a heavenly calling, consider that Jesus, the apostle and high priest of our confession . . . (3:1)

The lead phrase to this section of Hebrews explains why the text turns first to "a heavenly calling" as the distant destination and then examines who can take us there, namely, Jesus. These two points explain the call we receive.

WHAT IT SAYS

The Household of Faith

Although there will be other occasions when the writer will tell us more about the ultimate destination that Christians can expect, in this setting, he gathers his teaching around two figures of speech. The one is a "house," and the other, "rest."

> [Jesus] was faithful to the one who appointed him, just as Moses also "was faithful in all God's house." Yet Jesus is worthy of more glory than Moses, just as the builder of a house has more honor than the house itself. (For every house is built by someone, but the builder of all things is God.) Now Moses was faithful in all God's house as a servant, to testify to the things that would be spoken later. Christ, however, was faithful over God's house as a son, and we are his house if we hold firm the confidence and pride that belong to hope. (Hebrews 3:2-6)

We are told that, as a faithful son, Jesus is building a "house." We are not to think of Jesus constructing a building that Christians will occupy, but a people in whom God will dwell. As stated earlier, we may continue as sojourners and strangers in relation to the world but are no longer aliens to God when we become Christians (Ephesians 2:19-22). The result of people receiving that blessing is a "building."

The meaning of the term *house* can be understood from other passages. In such passages as 1 Peter 4:17, the same word translated in Hebrews 3:5-6 as "house" is translated as "household," where we are told the "time has come for judgment to begin with the household of God." So too in Hebrews 11:7, concerning Noah's "household." In a number of passages, when a human household and not God's household is mentioned (Acts 16:15; 18:8; 1 Timothy 3:4, 12; 5:14), the reference is to a "family" (in all probability an extended family including several generations and servants). In Hebrews 3, where Jesus is building a house, we are therefore to see a family as a result of what it is Christ is building, in the same way God built a new people through their deliverance from bondage in Egypt or exile in Babylonia. They who were "no people" became a people of God (1 Peter 2:10).

The word *house* also points back to the inclusiveness the ancient Hebrews tried to capture in the phrase "the children of Israel." Within the twelve tribes, it was their way of acknowledging some diversity within the people of God that the gracious and mighty acts of God created through history. We will find reasons elsewhere in Hebrews to read in this vision of a family a more explicitly inclusive quality of the people of God. The writer was eager to open up the possibilities of more than one ethnic group entering the household of faith. The epistle was a sustained appeal to Christians, who saw in the history of the Jewish people a full expression of God's work, to see that same divine presence among other people. The readers were invited to move outside their familiar confines and meet Jesus in new settings.

A Promised Rest

In Hebrews 3 and 4 we read of the "promised rest" for those in the household of faith, or the people of God. The vision of the writer of Hebrews looks backward and forward at the same time to describe the characteristics of the household of faith in that climactic moment. In looking back to the stories of creation, he reminds the reader of a living God who labors and rests (4:4). Rest was written into the human cycle of life by God, who took time for rest. Once every seven days, they enjoyed respite from their labor. However, the respite, established with surety in the creative acts of God, pointed ahead to a rest that God is still working toward! "So then, a sabbath rest still remains for the people of God" (4:9). Thus, the "heavenly call" for Christian readers included "rest" from the labors of the people of God. In their day, they may have found themselves struggling, trudging ahead against those who told them to turn back and forget the beckoning that made them restless for those promised distant destinations.

We are not to read *rest* in a negative sense. In Hebrews 12, we will see the promised peace and righteousness as outcomes of those who endure suffering as training (12:11). Peace and righteousness are not only promised gifts, they are also qualities Christians are asked to realize: "Pursue peace with everyone, and the holiness [an analogous term to righteousness] without which no one will see the Lord" (12:14). Thus the combination of peace and righteousness found in other sections of Hebrews can help us understand the rest that will ultimately come to Christians. We might translate *rest* as resolution of turmoil (peace) and rectifying wrong (righteousness or justice). Rest comes when we can personally live rightly without striving and socially when there is peace with justice. Christians therefore are called to be sojourners en route to peace where righteousness prevails.

Jesus as Apostle, Son, and Priest

We now consider the One who makes rest possible. The opening verse of Hebrews 3:1–5:10 begins by urging the readers to "consider . . . Jesus, the apostle and high priest of our confession." Immediately thereafter, the writer also speaks of Jesus as a son (3:6). Apostle, Son, and high priest are titles that describe the identity of Jesus in relation to the "heavenly calling" of rest for the household of faith. These characteristics of Jesus also tell us who we are and how we are to respond.

Jesus as Apostle
The reason why the title of apostle is appropriate for Jesus is the good news that he brings in the promise of peace (*shalom**)* with righteousness and justice (*zedek**)—that is, rest for the

household of faith (see Hebrews 7:1-2). Because an apostle conveys this message, we can regard this identity as a version of the prophetic figure the author uses again and again in explanations of the identity of Jesus as a communicator or an expression of God's intentions. Unlike the comparisons drawn between Jesus and superhuman media of communication in angels in 1:5–2:18, this comparison is between Jesus and human modes of divine communication, Moses and Joshua. As the contrasts are drawn, the author supplements his reference to Jesus as an apostle (3:1) with a description of Jesus as a son (3:6).

What is at stake is the focus of Christians who were reading the epistle. The figures of Moses and Joshua must have had a peculiar hold on their consciousness. And for good reasons. Moses, for example, reminded the early readers of the crucial events in their history that brought them into existence as the people of God. He led them out of the bondage of Egypt. They were no longer beasts of burden constructing pyramids for self-indulgent pharaohs. They were people, not tools. Furthermore, they were people of God, not owned by others who had designs for their lives that contradicted God's intentions for them.

Moses was also recalled for his faithful service to God in the face of a stubborn people who wished to return to Egypt instead of facing the rigors of the trek through the wilderness or coping with the challenges of moving into a promised land with all its dangers. While Moses may have continued beckoning his people to the Promised Land (3:18), they refused to move into the land when they had a chance at Kadesh (Numbers 13). They would not believe Moses, who said they were able to enter. Hence the writer of Hebrews speaks of their unbelief (Hebrews 3:19). They hardened their hearts (3:8, 15) to God's calling, and, by rebelling against God (3:16), went astray (3:10) and fell away from the living God (3:12). Although they heard the good news, they refused to follow or "know" God's way (3:10). This catalog of sins stands in stark contrast to the faithful Moses who remained a servant within the household of God.

Because Moses held out the promise of rest, he was appropriately compared to Jesus, who represented for the readers good news of rest for the household of faith. Both Moses and Jesus announced a distant destination. Hence Jesus was compared to Moses when the author called Jesus an apostle. Apostles, like prophets, tell us what God is doing and will accomplish. The author, however, was claiming that Jesus not only announces the good news but actually implements it. Although Moses could be admired as a faithful servant in the household of God, Jesus was a faithful son over the household of God (3:5-6). Moses could not take the children of Israel into the Promised Land. He died before he could lead them into it. Jesus, however, would take them into the promised rest, according to the author of Hebrews.

Jesus as Son

The reason for this claim appears in the author's understanding of the distinction between son and servant. A son was, among other things, a royal figure. As such, a son reigned and therefore could achieve the goals of his actions. A servant had no comparable capacities, duties, nor expectations. Even a faithful servant does not have a sure guarantee of succeeding. Only a faithful figure endowed with the capacities and responsibilities of a son can build a household or family that will reach that promised rest. As a faithful, though unsuccessful, servant, Moses can be profoundly admired as one of us. But it is only a faithful Son to whom we can finally yield our ultimate trust and definitive loyalties.[1]

The point is made in reference to Joshua. He took the succeeding generation of the children of Israel into the Promised Land. The writer had no intention of dismissing that achievement but insisted that entry into the Promised Land only pointed ahead to a greater promised rest.

As the records recall, even after they had entered the land God had promised to the children of Israel, they found it necessary to struggle, work, and even fight. The oppression and exploitation they left behind reappeared in new forms in Palestine. During the time of the judges, new forms of oppression appeared in the land of promise. During the time of nationhood, prophets cited numerous instances of Israelites exploiting their own people and the strangers within their gates. They saw the judgment of God against these inequities. They were eventually taken captive into another land. Therefore their entry into the Promised Land under Joshua did not produce the full rest God foretold in the sabbath. "So then, a sabbath rest still remains for the people of God; for those who enter God's rest also cease from their labors as God did from his" (4:9-10). "For if Joshua had given them rest, God would not speak later about another day" (4:8). Because the readers had not arrived at the ultimate destination, the writer urged, "Let us therefore make every effort to enter that rest" (4:11). Struggles remained before they could repose in peace with justice.

The comparisons between Jesus and the two historical figures of Moses and Joshua are an elaboration of the titles of Jesus as an apostle and Son. Jesus comes bearing the good news of a promised rest for the people of God. Unlike Moses, he will take the new people of God into that distant destination, and, unlike Joshua, he will lead them into that fuller, secure promised rest.

As in Hebrews 1:5–2:18, there is a basic reiteration of that ancient Jewish understanding of *davar,* the meaning of word and event, communication and action, promise and fulfillment. Jesus as an apostle indeed proclaims good news. He not only expresses God's intentions but will also accomplish them as only a Son can. In Hebrews 1:5–2:18, the author expresses this point in speaking of Jesus as a messenger or prophet and a Son; in Hebrews 3:1–5:10 this point is expressed in the twin figures of apostle and Son.

Jesus as High Priest

This section (3:1–5:10) contains another figure. Jesus is also a high priest. If we see in the figures of apostle and Son a promise of fulfillment, it is forward looking. When we come to the high priest, we are talking about the present experiences of that promise that are mediated to us in the present, even if this is not devoid of some further fulfillment in the future.

> Since, then, we have a great high priest who has passed
> through the heavens, Jesus, the Son of God, let us hold fast to

our confession. For we do not have a high priest who is unable to sympathize with our weaknesses, but we have one who in every respect has been tested as we are, yet without sin. Let us therefore approach the throne of grace with boldness, so that we may receive mercy and find grace to help in time of need.

Every high priest chosen from among mortals is put in charge of things pertaining to God on their behalf, to offer gifts and sacrifices for sins. He is able to deal gently with the ignorant and wayward, since he himself is subject to weakness; and because of this he must offer sacrifice for his own sins as well as for those of the people. (Hebrews 4:14–5:3)

In 1:5–2:18, Jesus as a priest (2:10-18) is introduced after the lofty picture of Jesus as the Son resplendent in the glories of a royal figure (1:5–2:9). In this section, the figures of Jesus as a priest and a Son point us to a distant destination where we will find rest from our labors (3:1–4:13). In both cases the closeness of Jesus, or the proximity of divine resources, is depicted through the figure of a high priest (2:17 and 4:14). In the earlier section, the oneness of Jesus as high priest with humanity is established by pointing to a common origin: "he himself likewise shared the same things. . . . he had to become like his brothers and sisters in every respect" (2:14, 17). In this section, the oneness is established by the way high priests are appointed and chosen rather than a status conferred automatically by birth. And even then, they had to be made effective by a certain mode of life. In the case of Jesus, his supplications and sufferings made him into "the source of eternal salvation for all who obey him" (5:9). The supplications of Jesus were characterized by "loud cries and tears" born of godly fear (5:7). Further, "although he was a Son, he learned obedience through what he suffered; and having been made perfect, he became the source of eternal salvation for all who obey him" (5:8-9).

In 2:17, we read that Jesus is a "merciful and faithful high priest." We have seen that Jesus will be a faithful Son capable of taking his people into the promised rest. Now we find out why. His abilities were not automatically conferred but learned. Because of the temptations he encountered (4:15 and 2:18), the struggles represented in the "loud cries and tears" of the supplications (5:7), and the sufferings endured (5:8 and 2:18), he can become merciful and will "deal gently with the ignorant and wayward" (5:2). Because of being one with us in learning obedience "we do not have a high priest who is unable to sympathize with our weaknesses, but we have one who in every respect has been tested as we are, yet without sin. Let us therefore approach the throne of grace with boldness, so that we may receive mercy and find grace to help in time of need" (4:15-16).

Our Response to Jesus and the Call

Throughout this section (3:1–5:10), the writer depicts the immediacy of a "dangerous opportunity." The writer says, "Today!" this great Jesus is close by (3:7, 15 and 4:7). At the same time, the implication is that "today" great judgment awaits those who do not take hold of the resources to move on. They could die in their wilderness, like the ancients "whose bodies fell in the wilderness" (3:17), if they did not struggle for peace with righteousness. A note of urgency rings through this section.

If Jesus as an apostle bearing good news calls for a response of faith, and Jesus as a Son calls for obedience as he leads us through the trek through the wilderness to the Promised Land, then Jesus as a high priest calls for confidence to draw near and receive mercy to help in time of need.

People who live with the faith and hope described here are endowed with sanctity of life. Becoming such a distinctive people means they are set apart from others in their environment. Holiness is characterized by being set apart (2 Corinthians 6:17). The longing of sojourners makes them different from others; hence, they are "outsiders," the "marginalized."

What It Means

Pressing Ahead in the Promised Land

We have seen how the writer reminded the readers that followers of Jesus would find he can make them into a people of God and lead them into the promised rest. They who were, in the eyes of others, "no people"—regarded to be beasts of burden or some lower grade of humanity or freak accidents of nature—would become a people. They would be "of God," not owned by some pretenders taking God's place. They would not be managed or manipulated by others, but become a people of God, a household of God.

The people of God would find the promised rest, a peace with righteousness. In personal terms this meant fulfillment in doing what was right, not inaction assumed in pious poses. In social terms, this meant justice pervading all God's creation, not order with unredressed exploitation.

The author reminded the audience that Moses and Joshua had not produced such a people and had not led them to such a promised rest. While there was no denying that both leaders deserved respect and appreciation, they had not fully accomplished what they had set out to achieve. Work remained. They had not fully become the people of God in the Promised Land. The author beckoned them to strive toward that calling and promise. They must move ahead. The God who fulfills the promise was accompanying them.

The points the writer made are applicable to the United States. We have had our Moses and our Joshua. We were delivered from bondage and have conquered the promised land. While we may live in the promised land of the modern world, much work remains. These claims make sense if we first recall the use of the biblical modes in our history, and second, survey elements in our situation that call us to push ahead even if we live in a promised land. These considerations will uncover an application of Hebrews 3:1–5:10 for our situation.

In the moment of our origins, we appealed to the period of biblical history that the writer of Hebrews used. On the day we issued our Declaration of Independence, July 4, 1776, the Continental Congress directed Benjamin Franklin, Thomas Jefferson, and John Adams to design a seal that would capture our identity. "Franklin proposed a picture of 'Moses lifting his hand and the Red Sea dividing, with Pharaoh, in his chariot being overwhelmed by the waters, and with a motto in great popular favor at the time, "Rebellion to tyrants is obedience to God." Jefferson suggested a 'representation of the children of Israel in the wilderness, led by a cloud by day and pillar of fire by night.'"[2]

We appealed to the biblical models as interpretations of our experiences and aspirations. We had leaders who delivered us from bondage as Moses had done, and we had our sojourn in the wilderness. In the great Westward Expansion, which is so important to the recital of our achievements, the Daniel Boones, the Lewis and Clarks, and the pioneers and cavalry that followed were our Joshuas leading us into the Promised Land.

The waves of immigrants who came from Europe and the Latinos who were involved in our nineteenth-century expansion—as well as the immense numbers of immigrants from Asia, the Pacific Islands, and the Americas in the twentieth century—also absorbed this ethos. We saw ourselves as sojourners like Abraham and Sarah leaving their homes or as immigrants in the Promised Land triumphing over hardship.

While millions of our forebears have moved us out of our bondage as Moses did, and others have bequeathed to us great gains in the Promised Land as Joshua did, we have not arrived at our destination in this society. The high calling we find in Hebrews articulates much of our natural aspirations. We long to become a people of God living in the promised rest pervaded with, according to, and in which things are right. We have not, for example, become "the land of the free and the home of the brave," as we sing in our national anthem. This is to say the obvious. However, a brief rehearsal of our situation placed alongside our hopes will deepen our appreciation of the calling to press ahead we find in Hebrews. The urgency of striving "to enter that rest" we read in Hebrews 4:11 will well up within us.

The description of where we essentially are in the US appears in the document *To Establish Justice, to Insure Domestic Tranquility.*[3] Although it was published in 1969, the intractable issues remain. The parallel between the vision in Hebrews for peace with righteousness and the title of this report of the National Commission on the

Causes and Prevention of Violence should be noted. The projections that the commission made in 1969 for our central cities and their connections with the suburbs depict what we experience today between metropolitan centers and outlying countrysides.[4]

> Central business districts in the heart of the city, surrounded by mixed areas of accelerating deterioration, will be particularly protected by large numbers of people shopping or working in commercial buildings during daytime hours, plus a substantial police presence, and will be largely deserted except for police patrols during night-time hours.
>
> High-rise apartment buildings and residential compounds protected by private guards and security devices will be fortified cells for upper-middle and high-income population living at prime locations in the city.
>
> Suburban neighborhoods, geographically far removed from the central city, will be protected mainly by economic homogeneity and by distance from population groups. . . .
>
> Lacking a sharp change in federal and state policies, ownership of guns will be almost universal in suburbs, homes will be fortified by an array of devices from window grills to electronic surveillance equipment, armed citizen volunteers in cars will supplement inadequate police patrols in neighborhoods closer to the central city. . . .
>
> High-speed, patrolled expressways will be sanitized corridors connecting safe areas, and private automobiles, taxicabs, and commercial vehicles will be routinely equipped with unbreakable glass, light armor, and other security features. . . . Armed guards will "ride shotgun" on all forms of public transportation.[5]

The segregation of our population centers and outlying areas has come true. Our fears and suspicions have produced a prison of protection. We are hardly living in "the land of the free and the home of the brave." Persisting inequalities and the scramble for diminishing resources contribute their share to this situation.

Enormous efforts have been extended and untold millions of dollars have been expended in the intervening years to "establish justice, insure domestic tranquility," as we have committed ourselves to do in the Preamble of the Constitution. The grim projections, however, have come true. Reflections upon the results of the struggles since 1969 on the basis of Asian American experiences have led to a distinct perspective. A particular understanding, which the reflections produce, will help us appreciate the work of Christ and our task found in Hebrews.

The history of Asian Americans also has been filled with those reminiscent of Moses leading us out of various bondages in our past. This society has allowed a certain amount of success to lighter-skinned racial minorities in this land of promise. That is, we have had our Joshuas.

As racial and ethnic minorities, however, we recognize the gains are still tokens and advances precarious. In times of national distress—either in grave military danger, unrelenting economic challenges, diplomatic setbacks, or threatening cultural invasions of alien values—racial and ethnic minorities become scapegoats. This society can turn us into the most accessible targets when it ventilates national frustration and fear. No amount of high-sounding pronouncements from churches or our legal documents and all generous gestures to the contrary have secured us against these dangers.

Reflections on these experiences and the dynamics in our present status, therefore, lead us to pay attention to the larger forces at work in this society as well as the fate of individuals in the interplay of these forces. Sobering estimates lead us to see the need of salvation from the currents of energies coursing through our society and the shifting winds of doctrine that can threaten our movements in this land of promise or respites in the safe harbors at home.

These situations give racial minorities grounds for a realistic estimate of the powers that reign over us. The subtle ethos that claims whites are superior and the colorful are children who must be taught or kept in their place still finds ever new and ingenious ways of asserting itself. Key individuals and numerous organizations have contributed their share. That many persons and institutions have offered kind gestures is not denied. However, the overriding impact of educational institutions, employment agencies, financial interests, industries, legislatures, judicial systems, law enforcers, and many, many more groups have played their varied roles in the divisive developments.

These groups and the forces that work in them have outwitted the best informed and outmaneuvered the most energetic of our well-meaning friends. We therefore appreciate the references in Hebrews to the host of lords operating against the best interests of humankind. The same situation exists in the struggle of women, working classes, and the developing nations, as it does in racial issues.

We may not speak with the same words today, but the good news in Hebrews arouses hope for racial minorities. We read in Hebrews of God in Christ destroying "the one who has the power of death, that is, the devil" (2:14). In the continuing drama of salvation, we are invited to join Christ who is putting the enemies (1:13) in subjection under his feet (2:8-9). A fuller picture of Jesus as the Lord of Hosts rising to reign over the "host of lords" (see Appendix) comes to us as good news. Christ is therefore the high priest from whom "we may receive mercy and find grace to help in time of need" (4:16).

By contrast, the posture of the predominately white denominations in the US is generally misguided. Far too many imagine themselves beginning from above, on top of the situation. They do not see how their admirable efforts to "establish justice, insure domestic tranquility" have been overruled in the fulfillment of predictions made in 1969. Acknowledging the operations of these forces greater than themselves sounds too paranoid or too fatalistic whether the issue is race, women's needs, lower classes of people, or the Third World. Thus, they frequently overlook the full capacities of the evil we combat. More importantly, they overlook the grand scope of the salvation accomplished in Jesus against these evils and the full range of the tasks he made possible.

Among their own people, the founders of the Republic had some glimpse of the efforts required for freedom. When overriding forces worked contrary to their legitimate aspirations, they said, "Rebellion to tyrants is obedience to God." They overturned abusive rulers. Our new nation went on to use some abusive and tyrannical tactics, however. The Bible was used as a justification. Up to this point in our history, the stories of conquest have justified the wars against Native Americans throughout the land and Hispanics in the Southwest. The lands beyond the Mississippi River had been deeded to us through treaties, we argued. It was the Promised Land. The older translations of Joshua and Judges that we were using suggested we could destroy occupants of the land who would resist our takeover. By some estimates, the Indian Wars that covered several decades in our history involved the slaughter of tens of millions of Native Americans, far exceeding the six million Jews exterminated by Nazis in the 1930s and 1940s.

Recent biblical studies, however, have made it impossible to use the stories of conquest in this fashion. A serious mistranslation has been discovered! What has been translated as "inhabitants " is more accurately translated as those who ruled abusively, oppressively, and therefore, illegitimately.[6] The story of the children of Israel finding a livable space and a secure place in the Promised Land, therefore, involved overturning the exploitative manipulators who ruled the land. They may have been inhabitants, but the battles were against a particular kind of occupant, namely, the tyrants. With the new translation, the story which Joshua and Judges now tell is the overturning of abusive forces that had no just claims for deciding actions adverse to the people.

This recent rereading of the period of Joshua and Judges drawn upon by the writers of Hebrews helps us recognize the wisdom of our founders concerning tyrants. Because the descendants of these founders see themselves on top and not working from below, today such options sound strange, if not frightful to them, even if it is a part of their heritage. References to the "devil," "enemies," and "tyrants" sound too exaggerated for their situations. From the perspective of marginalized minorities though, obedience to God's call to press ahead to the rest in the Promised Land means that we will begin from below to undermine the reign of principalities and powers who manage and manipulate, exploit or oppress. We must overturn them if they resist the reign of God that brings harmony and justice.

We are not only called to press ahead to the Promised Land as the examples of Moses and Joshua suggest. We are urged to press ahead in the land of promise because new forms of oppression can occur there. That is what the Book of Judges tells us. That is also what an early Christian, St. Cyprian of Antioch,* said: "While a Christian is honestly serving God, that Christian is a stranger even in his or her own state. We have been enjoined as strangers and sojourners to sojourn here but not to dwell here."[7] That is, we must press ahead to the rest that comes when peace with justice prevails.

In this section (3:1–5:10), the writer of Hebrews states an encouragement and a warning. Today we may press ahead toward a peace where all is right (3:17, 15; 4:7). Everything is ready. No waiting is necessary. The evil one has been defeated and Christ is righting wrongs. Woe be to those who do not avail themselves of this opportunity of pushing toward this distant destination with the pioneer of salvation. In the past, God allowed such foot-draggers to die in the wilderness of their day (3:17). The vision of the destination and the possibilities that the work of Christ produces compels us to move ahead, pressing for the righteous peace. Amen.

Suggestions for Reflection

1. Spend time reviewing what this chapter says about our "distant destination" as a "house" or "household," and as a "rest." Do the same for the identity of Jesus Christ as an "apostle," a "Son," and a "priest" and the responses we are invited to make. Are there responses with the prayers suggested in Chapter 1?

2. Discuss the claim that people in the US are still en route as the children of Israel were in their journey to the Promised Land. Which of the lingering challenges to "establish justice, insure domestic tranquility" do you feel are particularly important to

address? Do you feel our faith in Jesus Christ leads us to address these issues?

3. Read Hebrews 5:11–6:20 and study Chapter 5, "Points of Departure." After you have done so, consider whether the writer of this study book has followed an important saying, "All good Christians are good Jews," thus affirming contributions from Judaism. Or is he encouraging prejudice against Jews?

4. In order to prepare for "What It Means" in Chapter 5, "Points of Departure," examine "The Baptismal Covenant I," pages 33–39 in *The United Methodist Hymnal.* Reflect on the "Renunciation of Sin and Profession of Faith," as well as "Baptism With Laying On of Hands." Because of the ecumenical consensus on baptism, most other denominational baptismal rites will include the same acts.

Chapter 5

*Points of Departure:
Hebrews 5:11–6:20*

Introduction

The author of Hebrews has urged us to follow the pioneer of our salvation and alerted us to the potential distractions from other messengers. We have seen the distant destination of rest in the Promised Land for the household of faith (Hebrews 4:9-10). We have heard about some of the qualities of the priest who can provide what we need to proceed en route (2:10-18 and 4:14-16; see also 5:11). However, without being clear about what we must leave behind, we can be hampered from moving forward. Thus, the writer is specific about the points of departure for the sojourn (5:11–6:20). If the root metaphor of the wilderness sojourn helped us appreciate the destination of rest in the Promised Land for the household of faith, the same metaphor illustrates the points of departure in the Exodus from Egypt.

In this section, the writer moves us through three steps. He begins with an instruction (5:11–6:3), then offers a warning (6:4-8), and concludes with encouragements (6:9-20).

WHAT IT SAYS

The Process of Maturation
(Hebrews 5:11–6:3)

In the instruction (5:11–6:3) the process of maturation represents the central illustration:

> For though by this time you ought to be teachers, you need someone to teach you again the basic elements of the oracles of God. You need milk, not solid food; for everyone who lives on milk, being still an infant, is unskilled in the word of righteousness. But solid food is for the mature, for those whose faculties have been trained by practice to distinguish good from evil. (Hebrews 5:12-14)

The readers are compared to children who have not been weaned from milk. They have not learned to eat solid food. Their immaturity can also be likened to relearning the alphabet, the ABCs, as some translate the phrase "basic elements of the oracles of God." They confine themselves to the "basic teaching about Christ" (6:1). If they were mature they would have their "faculties . . . trained by practice to distinguish good from evil."

> Therefore let us go on toward perfection, leaving behind the basic teaching about Christ, and not laying again the foundation: repentance from dead works and faith toward God, instruction about baptisms, laying on of hands, resurrection of the dead, and eternal judgment. (Hebrews 6:1-2)

The suggestive notion of an alphabet mentioned by some translators helps us interpret the six topics the readers were urged to leave behind. They include (1) repentance from dead works, (2) faith toward God, (3) baptisms, (4) laying on of hands,* (5) resurrection, and (6) eternal judgment. Like letters in the alphabet, they were to be used to articulate words and, in turn, fuller messages in sentences, paragraphs, and so forth. The resulting utterances were far removed from the sound of individual letters. While using the elementary doctrines, or first principles, they were urged to move to something else. This applied to their Jewish past, as well as the first stages of their Christian experiences.

As we will note in several of the six topics mentioned, much of what God had done in Judaism was taking place in Jesus. Thus, the experiences and ideas associated with Judaism will help us understand what is happening in Christian experience. At the same time, however, the new and decisive work of Christ burst through those molds. Sole reliance upon Jewish background could not grasp fully what God was doing in Christ. Hence the writer's claim in Hebrews 7–10 that the Jewish priesthood, its laws, and its sacrifices became obsolete in Jesus. As a matter of fact, interpreting Jesus exclusively through Jewish heritage could result in treating of some of the work of Christ contemptuously and could even be compared to crucifying him afresh (6:6).

This basic concern about the help and hindrances of Jewish precedences appears at other points in Hebrews, as in the author's attempt to open the Jewish Christians' eyes to the saving acts of God revealed through Gentiles and their distinctive cultures. Hence, the writer said that the readers must move "outside the gate" where they had encamped themselves—they were to leave behind the usual modes of divine action in order to encounter God in new forms (13:11-12, RSV).

Another understanding of the alphabet can help. It refers to elementary teaching within Christianity itself. Contending for the faith (Jude 3) can mean we become contentious for the fundamentals of the faith. Stymieing our fuller development, fundamentals can impair our abilities to distinguish between good and evil (5:14) as we promote peace with rightness (3:1–5:10) in the most limited personal and individual terms.

We now turn to summarize the six "letters" in the alphabet of faith the author urges readers to use for other expressions of God's vast communications and activities.

Repentance From Dead Works

For the writer, "dead works" here and in 9:14 could refer to two lines of thought. First, it could refer to religious behavior that was unproductive, especially those outward behaviors that may have been prescribed once but were made obsolete with the coming of Christ. This emphasis on the ineffective priesthood (7:11), unproductive covenant (8:9), and the sacrifice that "cannot perfect the conscience of the worshiper" (9:9) are a central concern in this epistle. This emphasis is comparable to a point that appears in the teaching of Jesus. When he said in the Sermon on the Mount that people who practice their piety in order to be seen of others, "have received their reward," Jesus was speaking ironically. These people will be praised by their neighbors, but such emulation is empty compared to the acceptance that humble behavior would receive from God (Matthew 6:1-4).

There is a second kind of behavior associated with death. The sins of unbelief, rebellion, and hardness of heart led to death in the wilderness rather than rest in the Promised Land (Hebrews 3:17). The author reminded the readers that anyone "who has violated the law of Moses dies without mercy" (10:28) because "our God is a consuming fire" (12:29). This second interpretation is in line with other New Testament writers, such as Paul. He said, "the wages of sin is death" (Romans 6:23. See, too, 6:21 and 7:11). This is also in line with the teaching of the Old Testament concerning the consequences of sin (Genesis 3:3).

Whether it was unproductive action or sinful behavior, the elementary doctrines taught the people that repentance from these forms of "dead works" was required. Repentance included regret for a course of action and turning away from it. The writer was urging readers to leave behind the repentance known in Judaism, just as the Gospel writers urged in their recollections of John the Baptist. John's repentance, which was comparable to laying the ax on the roots of fruitless trees, was only preparation for the repentance evoked by Jesus who would bring judgment with unquenchable fire (Matthew 3:3, 6, 12). Within their Christian pilgrimage, repentance was but an entry to the preaching of Paul (Acts 20:21). Whether viewed as Jewish precedence or as Christian experience, repentance was clearly a point of departure from which one moved ahead.

Faith in God

If repentance is a turning away from dead works, faith is a move toward God. The negative precedes the positive. In contrast to dead works, faith is not a reliance on efforts that do not produce salvation, nor is it a line of behavior that leads to death. Faith is a yielding to God, a trust that renews life within us. The writer of the epistle has already called the reader's attention to the faith required in Christ, who represents a promise of rest (Hebrews 3–4). While this emphasis on faith is central to early Christians—"if you . . . believe in your heart . . . you will be saved" (Romans 10:9)—it is also found in Judaism. The Jews recognized Abraham as a forebear of all the faithful because he "believed the LORD; and the LORD reckoned it to him as righteousness" (Genesis 15:6). The prophet Habakkuk later announced "the righteous live by their faith" (Habakkuk 2:4).

The writer found in these fundamentals of the faith a potential impediment that hampers Christian growth into maturity. Here again, we may notice authentically Christian qualities in the foundational teachings but also recognize in them teachings from a Jewish past that might have thwarted the original readers from realizing fully what God had done in Christ along those same lines. It was not faith in God in general but faith in Christ that became the paramount concern.

Baptism

The word for baptism in this passage refers to Jewish practices of washing or ablutions* (Mark 7:4; Hebrews 9:10). Jewish Christians were very likely preoccupied with the tradition of ablutions that they had received. That tradition appeared, for example, in the opponents of Jesus who were troubled because the disciples failed to wash their hands as well as their utensils before they ate (Mark 7:2-5). To go beyond that perspective could mean the priority Jesus had in mind. "There is nothing outside a person that by going in can defile, but the things that come out are what defile" (Mark 7:15).

We can appreciate the change required within for good to come out of us, if we compare what John the Baptist offered in his baptism and what Jesus accomplished. John the Baptist offered a baptism of repentance that laid the ax to root out sin (Luke 3:9) and with water cleansed the people of their sins (Matthew 3:11; Mark 1:4). His emphasis recalled the word of God that Ezekiel proclaimed. "I will sprinkle clean water upon you, and you shall be clean from all your uncleannesses, and from all your idols I will cleanse you" (Ezekiel 36:25). Similarly, Zechariah proclaimed, "On that day a fountain shall be opened for the house of David and the inhabitants of Jerusalem, to cleanse them from sin and impurity" (Zechariah 13:1). By contrast, the baptism of Jesus did not only have the negative sense of dying with Christ to our sin, but also had the positive emphasis of being raised a new person and walking in newness of life (Romans 6:3-6). Putting away sins and putting on righteousness in many ways are listed in Ephesians 4:25, 32 and Colossians 3:5, 12.

Laying On of Hands

The same basic principle holds in the case of "laying on of hands" as in baptism. The practice was Christian but informed by Jewish precedence. An attachment to historical models without accepting new modes of that same basic work of God would have prevented these Jewish Christians from moving with God into new arenas of saving work.

Among the Jews, the rabbis ordained persons by laying on hands. This act repeated what Moses was asked by God to do about his successor. God said, "Take Joshua son of Nun, a man in whom is the spirit, and lay your hand upon him . . . [and] he laid his hands on him and commissioned him—as the Lord had directed" (Numbers 27:18, 23; Deuteronomy 34:9). The laying on of hands in the Jewish sacrificial rites could represent something quite different, namely, a passing of sins to the offering that was sacrificed (Leviticus 1:4; 3:2; 4:4; 8:14).

Early Christian illustrations of laying on of hands appear in the Acts of the Apostles. The act was associated with the descent of the Holy Spirit upon the person. Early converts may have believed in Jesus, but a laying on of hands added the anointing of the Holy Spirit (Acts 8:17). Ananias was instructed to lay his hand on Paul. Along with healing associated with laying on of hands (Mark 6:5; 16:18; Luke 4:40; Acts 28:8), the act also mediated the Holy Spirit upon Paul (Acts 9:12, 17).

The empowerment of the Spirit, however, was not an end in itself. The laying on of hands that communicated the Spirit also launched people into mission and service, just as the descent of the Spirit upon Jesus after his baptism eventually led to his ministry. In the case of Paul, he was commissioned to bear witness to Christ; in the case of Stephen and others, they were called to serve as deacons (Acts 6:6; 13:3; 1 Timothy 5:22 [see footnote in NRSV]; 2 Timothy 1:6) and other Christians received the gift of tongues and prophecy (1 Corinthians 14:2-3).

As might be surmised, the Jewish precedences illuminated the meaning of laying on of hands. It suggested a commissioning for services that the descent of the Holy Spirit would bring. It was not only an act that acknowledged the presence of that Spirit, as in the case of Moses recognizing the Spirit in Joshua, but the Jewish precedences suggested other acts that were no longer necessary if the death of Christ had made the offering of unblemished sacrifices obsolete.

As in the case of repentance, faith in God, and baptism, the precedences in Jewish communities were at once illuminating and potentially hampering. Distracting connotations could slip into the picture if they thought of the laying of hands on animals in the sacrifices, as noted earlier. It is no wonder then that the writer wished to move the readers ahead and use that illuminating heritage as a building block for further maturity. They were the letters in an alphabet, the ABCs, which they could use to express God's word more fully.

The baptism with water for repentance and faith, plus the laying on of hands, recalled for the early church an important sequence in God's actions in the baptism of Jesus (Mark 1:10) and the conversion of Gentiles (Acts 19:1-7). Many Christian denominations now highlight these two acts in baptismal rites.

Resurrection and Judgment

The early church knew that the Pharisees believed in resurrection (Acts 23:8). They were following such teachings as those in Isaiah 26:19 and Daniel 12:2. With the resurrection of Jesus Christ, however, the early church had much more to explore and experience. They could encounter the risen Christ as the apostle Paul did (Acts 9:5; 2 Corinthians 12:9). Interactions with the resurrected Christ confronted them with a mission (Luke 24:44-49; John 21:15-19). Joining Jesus Christ in his death and resurrection transformed believers (Galatians 2:20). The impact of the Resurrection was vast. It overthrew rulers and subjugated all things under Jesus Christ (1 Corinthians 15:24-28).

The early church also appropriated Jewish teaching concerning God's judgment that would separate evil from good (Daniel 7:9; Isaiah 33:22). The early church again had much more to explore in the culmination of God's mission on a grander scale (Matthew 25; 2 Peter 3:13; Revelation 22). The Jews and the Gentiles will be around God's throne with their distinct cultures (Revelation 7:1-9). Furthermore, the twelve gates into the New Jerusalem will be named after the twelve tribes of Israel (Revelation 21:12), and the Gentiles will bring the distinct glory of their cultures into the New Jerusalem (Revelation 21:24-26). The conversion of the Gentiles did not do away with their distinct identities and cultures. We should therefore celebrate new cultural expressions of the Christian faith.

Along with the foundations in repentance and faith, the instructions concerning baptisms, laying on of hands, resurrection, and judgment were seen as elementary principles. Those beginning their Christian faith were expected to know them and have had some experience of them. The writer saw them as essential; they were building blocks for something more. Or, to return to the illustration from language, they were the alphabets from which Christians could communicate more fully God's word and work, and communicate to others. Given the Jewish cast of so much of what lay behind them, the author was also anxious that the early Christians who saw God acting in Judaism would not confine God to those modes of actions of God in Christ and therefore be ready to move into other distinctive expressions of the same redemptive work of God.

Warning and Encouragement
(Hebrews 6:4-20)

As it has been observed in the introduction of this chapter, the author moved from instruction (5:11–6:3), through a warning (6:4-8), to encouragement (6:9-20). The latter two steps require some analysis.

For the warning, the writer recalled their exodus and their journeys in the wilderness (see also Hebrews 3:16-19):

> For it is impossible to restore again to repentance those who have once been enlightened, and have tasted the heavenly gift, and have shared in the Holy Spirit, and have tasted the goodness of the word of God and the powers of the age to come, and then have fallen away, since on their own they are crucifying again the Son of God and are holding him up to contempt. Ground that drinks up the rain falling on it repeatedly, and that produces a crop useful to those for whom it is cultivated, receives a blessing from God. But if it produces thorns and thistles, it is worthless and on the verge of being cursed; its end is to be burned over. (Hebrews 6:4-8)

The people who fell away from God were those who had experienced the deliverance from bondage in Egypt. Although they had experienced the mighty acts of God in the Exodus, they did not endure the rigors of the long haul to the Promised Land. They were nostalgic for the leeks of Egypt and did not like surviving on the manna God provided them in the desert en route to Canaan. Because they did not believe in the promises of God, they disobeyed God's command to enter the land. Thus, their "bodies fell in the wilderness" (3:17). In other words, although they experienced the goodness of God, they did not follow God, who beckoned to the promised fulfillment in the land of Canaan.

According to the writer of Hebrews, the readers experienced many good things associated with salvation. They had been enlightened, tasted the heavenly goodness of God's word and the powers of the age to come (6:4-5). But they were running into the danger of treating the work of Christ contemptuously and thereby committing apostasy.* What we saw earlier concerning repentance and faith, baptisms and laying on of hands, resurrection and judgment (6:2) illustrate one way Christ was treated contemptuously. His contributions were trivialized by reducing them to earlier works of God. God in Christ could be understood largely in terms of his own Jewish predecessors, but a lot more was happening. Jesus was making salvation available to all people. The failure to recognize this extension of God's work was nothing less than apostasy and was comparable to crucifying Jesus again. The writer compared the readers to a plot of ground that receives refreshing rain but produces useless thorns and thistles and not edible vegetation. Being worthless, the by-products only deserve to be cursed and burned (6:7-8).

Immediately following these threats and harsh warnings, the writer introduced assurances and encouragements. He was quite certain these threats would not apply to his readers.

The audience has not wholly apostatized.* They had built upon the elementary doctrines some measure of "work and the love that [they] showed for his sake in serving the saints" (6:10). While he was assured that their knowledge of the "first principles of God's word" (5:12, RSV) had produced some fruit and was not wholly characterized by "thorns and thistles," he still encouraged them to "the same diligence so as to realize the full assurance of hope to the very end" (6:11). It was not enough to do good deeds, but they were to be accompanied with earnestness characteristic of those who lived by faith in the promises mentioned earlier. They were to "make every effort to enter that rest" (4:11).

The basis of this hope was the promise of God, backed up with an oath. The readers were reminded of the patient faith of Abraham, who endured until God finally gave him and Sarah a son (6:13-15). He had borne the name that means "glorious father"—Abram. After his impatience had led him to try to realize God's promise through a handmaid instead of through his wife Sarah, he was given a new name—Abraham. No longer could he be called Abram "glorious father" but Abraham "father of many nations." Finally, late in life, he and his wife welcomed Isaac, the son of promise into their lives (Genesis 15–18; 21:1-7 and Romans 4:16-25).

God's sure promises illustrated by Abraham and Sarah were used as encouragements for Christians. As God's promises to Abraham and Sarah were backed up with an oath, so too God's promises through Christ are backed up with an oath. The author had in mind Psalm 110, which is so central to much of this epistle: "The LORD has sworn and will not change his mind" that a priest "according to the order of Melchizedek*" will reign forever, with righteousness and justice, and bring peace (Psalm 110:4). The promise and the oath represented a "sure and steadfast anchor of the soul" (6:19). That hope was tied to the fact that Jesus as a forerunner had already become a priest effectively mediating God's blessings.

What It Means

The emphases in Hebrews 5:11–6:20 can be applied to our situation. One has to do with the starting points and the other the departure or progress beyond them. The starting points make us outsiders or persons marginalized from the world. Progress beyond those points pushes us en route, or makes us migrants. We are therefore "outsiders en route" or "marginalized migrants."

Outsiders: Repentance and Faith

Not all of us who are active in churches can claim to have actually undergone repentance or acted in faith as could the original readers of Hebrews. We have not tasted the goodness of God and the power of the age to come. Nothing reminiscent of an exodus or deliverance from some bondage has occurred.

We may run around for the church, give generously, and even accept the teachings about the actual changes that can occur through the living presence of God. However, our "busy-ness" and considerable familiarity with the doctrines may not have made us close to a living God. God is a distant one who must be kept happy lest we suffer some vindictive reprisals for our sins.

One of the central messages of the United Methodist heritage is that repentance from dead works and trust in a gracious God actualize a living and active presence of God in our lives. This presence is struggling to come up to the surface.

We have recognized that confession of sin, which tells God where we actually are, is a crucial part of repentance. We are invited to tell God how dead our works are. They may be dead because they are empty or represent designs to manipulate the God who already wishes to act graciously. They may be dead because we injure or kill something deep within our souls or we destroy something in human interactions. To confess is to speak the same word that God has already announced concerning the persons we are and our actions. Speaking in full accord with God means our lives are attuned to God and hence in good relationship with God.

Repentance also involves a turning away from a course of action or a line of thought and turning toward God. This understanding places a heavy emphasis on the concrete actions that are involved in repentance. Should emotions accompany them, fine. Should there be regret, for example, or even remorse, fine. But emotions are the by-product and not themselves the sufficient ingredients that make repentance transform life. Changes come from stating who we are and what we have done through confession to God and turning away from that kind of life toward God. Faith as trust in, openness toward, and commitment to God becomes a natural act. Reliance upon and yielding to the activities of God within us realize the divine presence that renews, cleanses, and transforms.

Repentance and faith have become prominent in the baptismal rites of many denominations because of the ecumenical consensus in the last quarter of the twentieth century. Allowing for slight differences in the wording among denominations, we as United Methodists express and enact our repentance in a "Renunciation of Sin," and bear witness to our faith in a "Profession of Faith." The Renunciation sets us apart from the world around us. "Do you renounce the spiritual forces of wickedness, reject the evil powers of this world, . . . [and] accept the freedom and power God gives you?" The Renunciation follows what the apostle Paul asked, "Do you not know that all of us who have been baptized into Christ Jesus were baptized into his death?" (Romans 6:3). We reenacted the "burial" most effectively by being immersed in water. Dabbing water on the forehead is a safe and a very poor expression of that death to sin. "Our old self was crucified with him so that the body of sin might be destroyed, and we might no longer be enslaved to sin. . . . But if we have died with Christ, we believe that we will also live with him" (Romans 6:6, 8).

The baptismal rites coupled repentance in the "Renunciation of Sin and Profession of Faith" because death to sin makes us alive to God in faith. "Just as Christ was raised from the dead by the glory of the Father, so we too [can] walk in newness of life." (Romans 6:4).

Beyond baptism with water, the laying on of hands in the baptism signals an anointing of the Holy Spirit that empowers us for service. The United Methodist rite spells out concretely how we serve, namely, by joining that denomination as part of the church universal and pledging to participate in its mission by our prayers, presence, gifts, service, and witness.

In these ways baptism enables us to name our points of departure. Recognizing the decisive transition in our baptism, we do not re-baptize. Rather we undergo periodic baptismal renewals, because we need to continue repenting, believing, and being anointed afresh by the Holy Spirit.

En Route

We have noticed that we as Christians are expected to build on elementary experiences and teaching. As noted earlier, those "points of departure" are like letters in the alphabet that we build into words, sentences, and paragraphs in order to express our faith in new ways. The Epistle to the Hebrews urged Jewish

Christians to recognize the sanctity in new expressions of the faith unlike their own in the Gentile world.

That emphasis of recognizing sanctity in new and different forms is particularly relevant in our historical setting that we observed earlier in Chapter 2. God as the Migrant Worker is moving into new developments while creating new people and cultures and redeeming whatever goes awry in them. Christians are called to migrate with this God while working with their Creator and Redeemer.

Some Christians in the emerging Third Church are calling for fundamental changes in the forms our faith takes in this third millennium of Christianity. In a novel entitled *Silence,*[1] Shusaku Endo has illustrated these aspirations for basic changes. The Japanese Roman Catholic layperson urges Christians in his native land to adapt their faith to their unique settings. This is necessary because Christianity from Europe is comparable to a sapling planted in a swamp. The swamp of Japan will rot the roots and the leaves will wither. What remains is, at best, comparable to a butterfly in a spider's web. The spider will catch it and draw the life nourishment out of it. The butterfly that remains may be colorful and beautiful, but it is dead! In plain words, he is saying that European Christianity will not survive in Japan.

Endo remains a Christian. How he does this is found in the novel. Using a setting of Roman Catholics in sixteenth-century Japan, Endo depicts staunch Dominican missionaries apostatizing. They were rejecting a European brand of faith. They had relied on God to intervene in their dreadful persecutions and answer their prayer. God remained silent, hence the title of the novel.

Besides depicting this basic shift in their view of God, Endo shows them coming in touch with a very different Jesus. There is a growing contrast between the European portraits of Christ that sustained Father Rodriques in his heroic and sacrificial missionary endeavors, and the picture of Jesus he finally accepted in the *fumie.* The *fumie,* roughly translated, is a "picture we step upon." As an act of renunciation, Christians were asked to step on the plaque with a bronze face of Jesus. Whereas the European Jesus was pictured with a halo or bathed in light, the *fumie* Jesus was bordered in black. Unlike European pictures of Jesus, such as the Baroque paintings depicting divine figures as full forms, the Jesus of the *fumie* had sunken cheeks worn down by the thousands of feet that trampled on his face.

The European pictures of Jesus that the missionary recalled were beautiful, handsome, strong. The *fumie* Jesus was weak, emaciated, and ugly. Such was the Jesus who invited Father Rodriques to trample on him. When Father Rodriques finally stepped on the *fumie,* he bid farewell to the European understandings of Jesus and came in touch with the Japanese Jesus.

The face and other imagery in the novel are reminiscent of cultural forces at work in Japan that are largely indebted to Buddhism. Note how Japanese culture, with its Buddhist influences, has transformed the Christ that Endo says we meet there. Cultures influenced by Buddhism can speak of suffering and death in affirmative terms. Even suicide becomes a positive act in some forms of Buddhist influence, as distinct from martyrdom for a cause we may affirm.

By speaking of the fate of European and North American Christianity in Japan as a death of a sampling and the remains of a butterfly caught in a spider's web, Endo indicates fundamental changes occurring in the emergence of the Third Church in the third millennium. What we detected in Hebrews applies in our responses to Endo. We noted how Christians appealed with benefit to the Jewish practice of laying on of hands. It conveyed the empowerment of the Spirit that was foreshadowed in Judaism. It also recalled, however, transmitting sins to a scapegoat. The historical consequences of the work of Christ made that act obsolete. Thus, laying on of hands, while good, did have its misleading suggestions.

Endo suggests that our attraction to the Resurrection, in contrast to his attention to the Crucifixion, is sound but can become misleading. Our affirmation of the Resurrection obviously has Christian precedence, but our interpretation of the Resurrection has been influenced by powerful cultural forces that look for completeness in success, or in a hasty and wholesale solution. This means that, when it comes to Christians reliving the Resurrection in this life, we expect conspicuous transformations and big success stories. In our evangelism and mission, we expect thorough changes in others (but not ourselves). The racial minorities at home and the Third World people abroad, for example, are expected to manifest some fundamental changes. Generally they are asked to leave their cultural heritage and ethnic identity behind as they become similar to Christians in Europe and North America. While other forces may be at work, the pervasive coloring of this success orientation and expectations of changes in others have made it difficult for us to speak of resurrection to these people without unfortunate consequences.

The problems are most evident in the historic setting noted earlier. In a time when Christian initiative is passing into the Third World and a Third Church is emerging, we in the Second Church will be expected to undergo changes. It is not a time to be difficult and demanding. It is not too much to say some form of suffering will be involved.

Endo's focus on the Crucifixion is thus worth considering. The Jesus with sunken cheeks encountered in the darkness speaks to the depth of the pain we experience in being human. Meeting one who suffers changes can offer a way of uncovering sanctity in our historic setting and provide possibilities for saving interactions with people who express new brands of faith alien to us. The writer of Hebrews bid his readers appreciate the continuity with the past even in those who introduced a different kind of faith. Endo's witness helps us appropriate the reality of suffering and struggle we may have ignored in the biblical stories of Jesus.

Through Endo, for example, we can appreciate the important and frequently overlooked message of the New Testament that even the Resurrected One is recognized by his wounds (Luke 24:39; John 20:27). The Resurrection did not erase the scars incurred in faithful and costly service! Even the ascended Jesus is not simply resting on his laurels as victor in heaven but is interceding for us (Hebrews 7:25). If his earthly intercessions are any indications of his heavenly intercessions, he is offering prayers and supplications "with loud cries and tears" to God who is able (5:7). In other words, the ascended Jesus must be seen as participating with his brothers and sisters in their struggles and sufferings during their prolonged departure from our focus; it is connected to the biblical stories we may have overlooked.

No single people and no one cultural form can fully convey the richness of the total drama of divine action. What is urged in *Silence* is that we consider contributions from Japanese Christians as well as Christians in other continents and racial minorities at home. There are other analogies. As the distinctive contributions of women have a greater impact, the worship format, organizational structures and process, funding patterns, and other areas in the church can be expected to undergo changes. As persons with handicapping conditions sensitize the churches to new readings of the Bible and more humane use of symbols for salvation, our faith will also undergo changes in expression. Persons with sexual orientations that vary from that of the majority have already altered our theological outlook despite our resistance.

What we observe now is the way the writer of Hebrews tells us that we leave behind some treasured matters when we become sojourners who are en route. We have already observed the writer's warnings against distractions that may lead us astray (Chapter 3), as we have noted his picture of the distant destination (Chapter 4). We have concluded his reading of what we must depart from if we are to press ahead with God the Migrant Worker (Chapter 5). We will turn next to the sustenance for outsiders who are en route (Chapter 6) and the stamina that results for these sojourners (Chapter 7).

Suggestions for Reflection

1. Explore in small groups or as one group the meanings that repentance, faith, baptism, laying on of hands, resurrection, and judgment had for the readers of Hebrews, as summarized in this study. Reflect on whether your experiences are described by some of these phrases. Use the biblical references.

2. Have the leader play the role of a liturgist in baptism and ask the questions. Then, have the group respond with the "Renunciation of Sin and Profession of Faith." Do this as if individuals in the group were renewing their baptism as they continue en route on the journey of faith. Share together what you need to leave behind, as well as specific ways you will add tangible expressions to your faith.

3. Have the leader extend her or his hand over someone in the group and say the words for Laying on of Hands, "The Holy Spirit work within you, that being born through water and the Spirit you may be a faithful disciple of Jesus Christ," or a variation from another denomination. How well do those words express the biblical references to laying on of hands in "What It Says"?

4. In preparing for the next session, gain confidence in reading Scripture for yourself. Read the passage several times, then the text, before you reflect on what the Bible is saying to you. You will begin to discover a new ability to hear God's messages and should be finding means of responding through the use of the outline of prayer (page 3).

Chapter 6

Sustenance En Route: Hebrews 7–10

Introduction

The ancient Greek philosopher Plato described an ideal society in his *Republic*. For him, the most desirable ruler was a king who was a philosopher. For the writer of Hebrews, it is a king who is a priest, " 'King Melchizedek of Salem, priest of the Most High God,' . . . His name, in the first place, means 'king of righteousness'; next he is also king of Salem, that is, 'king of peace' " (7:1-2).

Readers in the United States are likely to have problems with that proposal on two counts. First, a kingly figure sounds outdated and hardly desirable. We live in a society that associates evil with kings and finds male and hierarchical models unduly restrictive. We might read references to that royal figure as one who reigns with righteousness and justice and thus makes peace possible. And yet, the word *reign* can raise problems because it suggests one who dominates. We might therefore think of Melchizedek, king of Salem, as the one who makes wholeness or peace pervasive because righteousness and justice are permeating the situation. This is what the kingdom of God has meant in the Bible.

Second, mention of a priest may be unfortunate. In a society dominated with a Protestant ethos, priests recall religious figures who are elitist. Hence we speak of our religious leaders among

Protestants as ministers or pastors. If communicating the spoken word is important, we call them preachers. The content of this section may help overcome our reluctance to see positive values in priests. In Hebrews 7–10, we find in Jesus a different kind of priest. The new priesthood of Jesus is described in Hebrews 7, with the new covenant he brings in Chapter 8, and the effective work he accomplished in Chapters 9–10. In "What It Says," more space will be devoted to the priesthood than to the covenant and sacrifice.

What It Says

A Priest Perfected and Permanent
(Hebrews 7)

In Hebrews 7, we read about the superiority of the priesthood of Jesus and how it was established. Similarities between Melchizedek and Jesus illustrate the superiority. This illustration recalls earlier discussions and will help us understand how the author concluded that Jesus was perfected and thus became a permanent priest.

To illustrate the superiority of Melchizedek, and therefore of Jesus, the writer alluded to that incident in Genesis 14:20 where Abraham offered a tribute to Melchizedek.

> See how great he is! Even Abraham the patriarch gave him a tenth of the spoils. And those descendants of Levi who receive the priestly office have a commandment in the law to collect tithes from the people, that is, from their kindred, though these also are descended from Abraham. But this man, who does not belong to their ancestry, collected tithes from Abraham and blessed him who had received the promises. It is beyond dispute that the inferior is blessed by the superior. In the one case, tithes are received by those who are mortal; in the other, by one of whom it is testified that he lives. One might even say that Levi himself, who receives tithes, paid tithes through Abraham, for he was still in the loins of his ancestor when Melchizedek met him. (Hebrews 7:4-10)

The gift of the tithe suggested that Abraham acknowledged that Melchizedek was a superior. Thus, if Jesus is a priest after the order of Melchizedek (5:6, 10), and if Abraham offered a tithe to Melchizedek, that indicates that Jesus is superior to Abraham, including the priests who came from his lineage. Such line of argument may not be convincing to moderns because we see ourselves as individuals without such connections, until we think of the way we speak of our Pilgrim forebears or our founding fathers and mothers. Such connections between Melchizedek and Jesus, which reach across the centuries, seem unreal, just as connections between Abraham and Levi (who was in the loins of Abraham) seem unreal.

For the writer and his audience, the lineage was real and implications could be drawn from such facts. The gift of a tithe from Abraham to Melchizedek established the superiority of that priestly king and descendants in his order, including Jesus.

Jesus was worthy of attention because he is a "priest forever according to the order of Melchizedek" (Psalm 110:4). The permanence of a priest no doubt sounds like an abstract claim about a static quality. The contents of the epistle here, and elsewhere, help us make this comparison more like a vital message of hope.

To begin with, the passage speaks of an oath that made him permanent (7:16-17, 21). A process is suggested, that is, he is made; and a promise is involved, that is, an oath is uttered. We will explain the process of making Jesus a priest forever, before explaining what is meant by an oath.

We might compare the process of making Jesus a priest forever to the process mentioned in John 1:12-13, where we are told the way we become children of God.

> But to all who received him, who believed in his name, he gave power to become children of God, who were born, not of blood or of the will of the flesh or of the will of man, but of God. (John 1:12-13)

The process of rebirth, which makes us children of God, does not happen automatically because we are physically born into a

Christian family ("not of blood"), nor of natural inclination ("will of the flesh"). Nor does our decision or someone else's ("will of man") make us into children of God. This process is "of God," and it occurs when we trust in that Name or the Person who is described by such names as loving, merciful, and able. When we believe in that God as manifested in Jesus we will "become children of God."

In the way that John distinguished Christian rebirth from physical parentage, so too the writer of Hebrews was anxious to say Jesus became or was made into a priest after the order of Melchizedek. Thus, his spiritual lineage was traceable to Melchizedek, although his biological ancestry was traceable to the tribe of Judah (7:14). He was made into a priest, not by physical descent as the Levitical priests, who were conferred that status by virtue of birth (7:16). Jesus was appointed by God to be a priest (5:5). Reference to an appointment is another way to speak of a promise backed up with an oath.

We have read earlier how Jesus was made a priest. He lived through certain trials and temptations and thus became a "merciful and faithful high priest" (2:17), just as believers undergo a process of rebirth before they become children of God in the full sense of that word. Jesus became such a compassionate priest by learning obedience like any other human being (see Hebrews 2:9, 18):

> Although he was a Son, he learned obedience through what he suffered; and having been made perfect, he became the source of eternal salvation for all who obey him, having been designated by God a high priest according to the order of Melchizedek. (Hebrews 5:8-10)

In taking death upon himself for everyone (2:9), he destroyed "the one who has the power of death, that is, the devil," and thereby he is able to "free those who all their lives were held in slavery by the fear of death" (2:14-15). This conquest of death makes it possible for the writer to say, "he lives" (7:8) "through the power of an indestructible life" (7:16). The indestructible life that works in this priest means that "he holds his priesthood permanently, because he continues forever" (7:24). The permanence is thus not a status achieved and simply held, but means "he is able for all time to save those who approach God through him" (7:25). A saving ministry is launched and insured; a static condition is not simply arranged. Later, when we read, "Jesus Christ is the same yesterday and today and forever" (13:8), we should read it in an active way and not as an abstraction we can admire as spectators. Jesus can save all sorts of people and under all conditions.

Thus, when the Lord swore that Jesus is a priest forever after the order of Melchizedek, it was a promise backed with an oath. With God's resolute action and faithfulness undergirding him, Jesus learned through suffering and became a high priest forever. The ingredients of this salvation (Hebrews 8) and further explanations of its foundations (Hebrews 9–10) are yet to be introduced. In the meantime, Hebrews 7 makes the claim that Jesus is a superior priest because he became one who could save humankind in all situations.

A New Covenant
(Hebrews 8)

Because perfection was not attainable through the Levitical priesthood, there was a need for a further one that we find in Jesus (7:11). With "a change in the priesthood, there is necessarily a change in the law as well" (7:12). "An earlier commandment" is set aside "because it was weak and ineffectual (for the law made nothing perfect)" (7:18-19). In Hebrews 8, Jesus is described as the mediator of a better covenant. An allusion to the Book of Jeremiah illustrates the new law, commandment, and covenant Jesus brings:

> This is the covenant that I will make with the house of Israel
>   after those days, says the Lord:
> I will put my laws in their minds,
>   and write them on their hearts,
> and I will be their God,
>   and they shall be my people.
> And they shall not teach one another
>   or say to each other "Know the Lord,"
> for they shall all know me,
>   from the least of them to the greatest.

> For I will be merciful toward their iniquities,
>   and I will remember their sins no more."
> (Hebrews 8:10-12; from Jeremiah 31:33-34)

Three major features of this covenant should be noticed. First, people will have a new law written in their very nature. The intentions of God for them will guide them, not some injunctions and commandments imposed on them by others who may have interests alien to the needs of people. Not being owned by others and living out God's will for them, these people will be God's people, not someone else's. Second, under such circumstances, people will not need to encourage others to know God. To know God will mean to be in intimate relationship with God rather than to have some order or command alien to God intervening between people and their God. Third, iniquities will be forgiven. Those prohibitions or directives that they may have violated will be forgiven. All three of these gifts point in the direction of purifying and perfecting the people, which, the writer of Hebrews said, Christ accomplished.

A Sufficient Sacrifice
(Hebrews 9–10)

Up to this point (Hebrews 7–8) in this section, the author has compared Jesus to Melchizedek, the changing Levitical priests, and the old covenant. In Hebrews 9–10, further comparisons with priests and their sacrifices help the writer elaborate on the identity and accomplishments of Jesus.

The comparisons draw on illustrations associated with the sojourn of the children of Israel in the wilderness. In Hebrews 3–6, when Jesus was compared to Moses and Joshua, the resources were similar. In this portion of the epistle, the author refers to sacrifices during the Day of Atonement (Leviticus 16) that were conducted originally in the Tabernacle in the wilderness. (See Exodus 25:10–26:37 for a description of the Tabernacle.) The reference is not to the Temple in Jerusalem, although some of the symbols and practices were continued in that later setting. His references are not always precise, but they are sufficiently close to help him illustrate what he wants to say about Jesus. What Jesus has accomplished makes him worthy of being followed and trusted.

Several features of the Tabernacle are described in Hebrews 9:1-5. There was an outer area called the Holy Place and an inner area called the Holy of Holies. The latter contained the throne of mercy atop the ark of the covenant. The Holy Place was separated from the Holy of Holies by a curtain. While priests could regularly enter the Holy Place, the Holy of Holies was entered only by the high priest, and that only happened once a year during the Day of Atonement. Entrance required sacrifices that cleansed the high priest of his own sins and purified the people of their errors. So long as the entrance into the Holy of Holies was restricted, coming close to God's mercy was limited to special occasions and restricted to the high priest. The restricted entrance reminded people that it was only limited in its effects (it symbolized the present age). This fact helped the author illustrate the work that remained for Jesus to do.

The Tabernacle depicted on earth what people felt was true in their relations with God. God was out of reach of people because their sins had alienated them from God. The shedding of blood by animals indicated something of what was necessary for purification (9:15-21). "Indeed, under the law almost everything is purified with blood, and without the shedding of blood there is no forgiveness of sins" (9:22).

Jesus did not make an offering with the blood of animals but with his own, as one who was without blemish. If the blood of animals could only purify the flesh (9:13), the blood of one who was without blemish could purify the consciences of people from dead works so that they could serve the living God (9:14). Because of the adequacy of the sacrifice Jesus offered, there would be no need for repeated sacrifices in the future (9:23–10:13). Christ offered the "full, perfect, and sufficient sacrifice for the sins of the whole world," as we once prayed during Holy Communion.[1]

Such is the meaning of the contrast between the offerings. On the one hand, the priesthood during the sojourn in the wilderness made offerings "repeatedly" (9:25-26), "continually"

(10:1), and "year after year" (10:3). On the other hand, Jesus offered a "single sacrifice" (10:12) "once for all" (9:26, 28; 10:10).

In addition to the differences in the sacrifice made in the blood that was shed, there was a difference in the place where it was offered. In the case of the earthly priest, it was offered on the mercy seat atop the ark within the Holy of Holies. This depicted something of what would be done in Christ. Jesus went into the very "presence of God on our behalf" (9:24; 10:11-12), so that we may approach the throne of grace (4:16). The author reminded readers that "when Christ had offered for all time a single sacrifice for sins, 'he sat down at the right hand of God,' and since then has been waiting 'until his enemies should be made a footstool for his feet'" (10:12-13).[2] The priest who offered a sacrifice for sin was seated (a royal position) with God. The priest was also a king.

If Jesus as priest and king offers a sufficient sacrifice and is seated with God until the enemies are subjugated to God, what are the consequences? The covenant is fulfilled. Two major features of the new covenant are promised in Hebrews 10:16-17, namely, the writing of the law within and the forgiveness of sins.

> "This is the covenant that I will make with them
>   after those days, says the Lord:
> I will put my laws in their hearts,
>   and I will write them on their minds,"
> [the Holy Spirit] also adds,
>   "I will remember their sins and their lawless deeds no more."
> (Hebrews 10:16-17)

The priestly sacrifice purifies the people of their sins (9:13-14). Being cleansed, they are sanctified (10:10). In addition to that, they are perfected because the reigning one is working to bring all under subjection to God's will. Perfection is another way of saying humankind is changed so that the very law of God is written into their nature. "For by a single offering he has perfected for all time those who are sanctified" (10:14). By contrast, the old priesthood, covenant, and sacrifices could not perfect people. "The law made nothing perfect" (7:19). "Gifts and sacrifices [were] offered [in the old sacrifices] that cannot perfect the conscience of the worshiper" (9:9).

In Hebrews 10:19-25, two clauses begin with the word "since" (10:19, 21); three clauses begin with the phrase "let us" (10:22, 23, 24). The clauses that begin with "since" remind us of what the priest-king has accomplished: the sacrifices of Jesus have made God readily accessible and he is one who reigns "over the house [household] of God" (10:19-21). Since Jesus had made a new and living way, approach to God becomes accessible. Our writer says, "Let us approach [God]" (10:22). Since the reigning one is still working to bring all under subjection to God's will, he says, "Let us hold fast to the confession of our hope without wavering, for he who has promised is faithful" (10:23). Finally, since the work of Jesus has already made us "perfect" in some sense of the word, he says, "Let us consider how to provoke one another to love and good deeds" (10:24).

A warning (10:26-31) and an encouragement (10:32-39) to practice good works follows.[3] Now that more grounds for accepting God's work in Christ have been further elaborated, the warning becomes more threatening. Passing up a conspicuously greater gift is comparable to pouring judgment upon ourselves. Thus, to spurn the Son of God, profane his blood, and outrage the Spirit will mean "there no longer remains a sacrifice for sins, but a fearful prospect of judgment, and a fury of fire that will consume the adversaries. . . . It is a fearful thing to fall into the hands of the living God" (10:26-27, 31).

Following the warning is an encouragement to "hold fast the confession of our hope" and "provoke one another to love and good deeds" (10:23, 24). The writer recalls them to remember their "hard struggle with sufferings" (10:32), a fuller elaboration on striving to enter rest (4:11). Suffering took such forms as abuse, affliction, and the plundering of their property (10:33-34). Struggling will continue to mean that they are to hold fast to their confidence with endurance. They are urged to press ahead rather than shrink back (10:35-39). For the writer, this encouragement to hold fast to their confession in good works, or of encouraging hard struggles despite suffering, is a major ingredient of faith.

Summary

Jesus is a priest forever (Hebrews 7). As such "he is able for all time to save" (7:25). That salvation is summarized in a new covenant: forgiveness of sins, transformation of people with the laws of God written into their nature, and humankind becoming a people of God and not tools or puppets of lesser pretenders to God's reign (Hebrews 8). All of this is possible because of the sacrificial death of Jesus. The priestly-royal Jesus also has a prophetic role of challenging us to do God's will (Hebrews 9–10).

WHAT IT MEANS

Sustenance for Sojourners

Up to this point, the application of Hebrews to our current situation has uncovered grounds for Christian identity and calling as outsiders who are en route. In exploring the relevance Hebrews 7–10 has for us, we will trace the sustenance that these marginalized migrants find in the Christ who forgives sins, writes a new law in our nature, and perfects them as a people of God (Hebrews 8:8-10). These acts correspond to the priest, prophet, and royal figure associated with Jesus in several points of the epistle. Descriptions of the ingredients of the new covenant in contemporary terms may help readers recognize similar actions of Christ in their lives, or these descriptions may point them in the direction where they may appropriate these gifts from God.

Forgiveness as Acceptance

In the United Methodist heritage, forgiveness has been seen in large measure as a divine acceptance in which the Spirit bears witness with our spirit that we are children of God (Romans 8:16). When John Wesley experienced his heart-warming acceptance, he became an effective instrument of a revival that spread widely.

The heritage remains strong within The United Methodist Church. Three expressions brought this home to me in recent years. The first appeared in the minutes of consultations conducted by the Health and Welfare Division of the General Board of Global Ministries in preparation for statements such as the 1980 General Conference Resolution on "The Church and Persons with Mental, Physical, and/or Psychologically Handicapping Conditions." It was clear in reading the witness at the consultations that those who have provided imaginative and faithful ministry in this arena have found in the inner witness of the Spirit a turning point in their lives.

Society may claim persons with handicapping conditions are the result of their mother's sinful alcoholism, or the outcome of a doctor's malpractice, or distorted creations of blind forces in nature, or the deformed consequences of a crazy auto accident. Whatever may have been involved, and regardless of the classifications society may place on them, persons with handicapping conditions have heard a word from God. They are children of God! Therefore they have a ministry as all others who trust in Christ.

While I was teaching a course on United Methodist history, doctrine, and polity, women seeking ordination talked about their calling to ministry. The words they had heard from society had cut them deeply. Some had been told that women who lead groups are comparable to sorceresses or witches who stir up trouble. They did not listen to these words, however. Essay after essay testified to another word they trusted: the inner witness of the Spirit called them people of God! That gracious word of acceptance, despite the rejection they may have encountered, had transformed their lives. They sought a ministry that would release that same witness of the Spirit in others, regardless of the rejection involved.

The same holds true in the struggles of racial and ethnic minorities. In the particular case of Japanese Americans, many of us have heard derogatory names that we find difficult to write about. There have been other classifications that have had drastic consequences. During World War II, our immigrant parents who were not allowed to become naturalized citizens were put in categories such as "enemy aliens." As the hysteria of war mounted, they further classified all Japanese Americans as "national security risks." Many of our fathers were arrested without charges and imprisoned without a trial or sentence. They were detained in Bismark, North Dakota, to investigate them and try to establish possible grounds for incarceration. No saboteurs or espionage agents were found.

In the meantime, their detention served a convenient purpose. It has become clear that they were removed from our communities because officials feared they might foment resistance to the mass imprisonment of the Japanese American population along the Pacific Coast. The majority of the 110,000 placed in America's concentration camps were citizens who were denied a trial by a jury of peers.

These events, which go back several decades, are not recalled to evoke guilt from those who might have prevented it. What is important to notice is the drastic consequences of using such labels as "enemy aliens" and "national security risks." They illustrate the ominous potential of comparable categories we impose on other racial minorities, the handicapped, or persons with sexual orientations different from our norm.

In the case of racial minorities, society may have called us a lower grade of humanity, throwbacks in the evolutionary process, nuisances, or troublemakers; but we testify to God as Spirit, who is bearing witness with our spirit. We who were no people, have become a people (1 Peter 2:10)! Because of the trusting in that word from God, no human utterances can in the end prevail even when they may inflict deep wounds.

For some readers, the emphasis on the inner witness of the Spirit may sound like a watered-down version of justification. The acceptance of God in the face of a pervasive neglect or rejection by others remains, however, a dominant note in the gospel within our tradition. It has converted an impediment into an asset among persons otherwise marginalized.

Writing a New Law Within

In the new covenant that Christ brought, the writer of Hebrews tells us, the law of God will be written in our very nature. This could mean that there will not be a disparity between the law of our behavior and the will of God. Our desires and God's intentions will coincide. Thus, no one will need to tell us how we should behave.

While this reading summarizes a basic meaning of the new covenant we have examined in Hebrews 8, it misses the implications for the readers of the epistle. Within the context of the concerns expressed by the writer, he was trying to tell the Hebrews that new laws written in the very make-up of people render old ones obsolete. The old law he had in mind was the one God gave to the Jewish people. Living in an age when Jewish Christians were interacting with Gentile Christians with the complex mix of cultures in the Hellenistic world, these Christians were hearing a strong challenge. The new law within the people that Jewish Christians would encounter among Gentile Christians could be very different expressions of God's will. Given that fact, it had become inappropriate for people in one cultural expression of Christianity to tell other people how their faith should be expressed.

Those who have experienced the inner witness of the Spirit that they are people of God, despite the uniqueness that others found so difficult to affirm, have taken this second step. They have recognized the will of God in their uniqueness. They see the new, distinctive law written within them as a gift that requires cultivating and results in sharing. These persons can face the danger of foisting their identities on others, but such is the risk of testifying to the fullness of God's created order.

Those who move with the Migrant Worker will bear witness to sanctity where others have seen paganism, evil, and much worse. Like Jacob, they will discover a ladder in the desert wastelands with messengers moving up to heaven and descending to the earth. A place where God did not seem to be present turned out to be the very house of God, a gate to heaven (Genesis 28:10-22). This reference to the immediacy of God in unexpected places leads us to explore the third quality of the covenant in our situation.

Knowledge of God

As we noted earlier, to know God is to enter a close relationship with the divine. This interpretation of knowing has been used to describe sexual intercourse, such as in the observation in Genesis 4:1 in the King James Version that "Adam knew Eve . . . and she conceived."

Knowing therefore implies a very close relationship. To speak of a relationship with God as a form of knowing is to suggest that nothing is interfering between such persons and God. Such is the perfection John Wesley had in mind. Given the focus in this context of the epistle upon the law, it is natural to consider the way laws that are alien to people can cloud their relationship to God. Inappropriate expectations, or unrealistic demands, can come between a person and the fulfillment God intended. When a person tries to be someone that God did not intend, that person can be sent on a trajectory that misses the avenue God intends for them.

The groups mentioned earlier can make sense of such a reading—persons with handicapping conditions, women who have become aware of potential contributions that society urges they repress, and racial and ethnic minorities with their unique cultures. They all know the way alien expectations interfere with their relationship with God. In addition, these laws or expectations have the backing of prominent individuals in key places with further support of crucial institutions that affect their lives. They turn expectations into forceful ordinances. Violations are punishable in hurtful ways. These practices are sometimes sanctioned by the church as well.

It becomes appropriate to speak of a host of lords managing and manipulating the persons who are different and know they are marginalized. The principalities and powers gather momentum, and well-meaning people cannot reverse this tide by themselves, no matter how educated, respectfully employed, wealthy, or prominent. They are outwitted and outmaneuvered by them as well.

The conditions that have been described in the first two points mitigate these circumstances and introduce momentary experiences of immediate relationship to God. They are the first fruits of the Spirit. God intends that more will happen and that this host of lords will not intervene in the relation between the Creator and the creatures. We have observed in other parts of Hebrews that God in Christ is subjugating these "enemies" and their demonic work of destruction (Hebrews 2:14-18). The one who has the power of an indestructible life will prevail over the death of budding forms of human life. As God redeems us from the reign of principalities and powers, we can come into a union with God. We can become people of God, not owned by those who would turn people into beasts of burden or stepping stones to advance the alien interest of the host of lords.

Summary

Our faith can marginalize us and make us outsiders to the world. We are told of an acceptance of God that weakens, if not neutralizes, the destructive powers of the rejection we encounter. Further, God has given us unique identities that we can actualize in our lives. Finally, this can happen with greater realization as we are freed from the domination of those forces that have separated us from God's best intentions. These gifts of the new covenant describe the sustenance extended to the sojourners. Persevering faith in such a gracious God will be required if outsiders are to prevail amidst the forthcoming resistance encountered in pressing ahead.

Suggestions for Reflection

1. Ask participants to state what is happening to them as they read the Bible, reflect on it, and respond to it in prayer to God. Encourage the citation and reading of specific passages.

2. Summarize in your own words what was said in the section on "A Priest Perfected and Permanent." Use specific scriptural passages that express qualities in Jesus that are particularly important. Do the same for "A New Covenant" and "A Sufficient Sacrifice," recognizing that some overlap appears in the text.

3. Review the acts of salvation mentioned in this section: the way God justifies us, sanctifies us, and makes us into a people of God. Share your understanding and experiences of the new covenant with others.

4. In preparation for the next session, remember a goal in the process of study: sharing your understanding with others encourages confidence in grasping God's message in the Bible. The passage for the next session includes one of the more familiar ones in the Bible, Hebrews 11:1–12:2.

Chapter 7

The Unrelenting Sojourners: Hebrews 11–13

Introduction

The author of the Epistle to the Hebrews has completed an encouragement of the readers (10:32–39). He has urged them to hold fast to their hope amidst their struggles and suffering. In Hebrews 11 the immediate and most conspicuous references are to faith. The models of faith are characterized primarily by struggle, suffering, and hope. In Hebrews 12 discipline is mentioned and the further word on the destination of Christians is added. Struggle, suffering, and hope are still within view. Finally, in Hebrews 13, when the author becomes specific as to the outcome of discipline in good works, the conditions that make that kind of living possible are still struggle, suffering, and hope. From Chapters 11–13, the visibility of these concepts moves progressively from the foreground to the background, but they are still crucial at the end of the Book of Hebrews.

The analyses in this chapter will describe the persevering faith in Hebrews 11:1–12:2 and the pilgrimage of the faithful in Hebrews 12:3–13:25. Together they depict the unrelenting sojourners.

WHAT IT SAYS

A Persevering Faith
(Hebrews 11:1–12:2)

Major themes in this treatment of faith in Hebrews 11:1–12:2 are summarized in the opening verses.

> Now faith is the assurance of things hoped for, the conviction of things not seen. Indeed, by faith our ancestors received approval. (Hebrews 11:1-2)

Different translations of the Bible emphasize different qualities of faith. By speaking of assurance and conviction, the New Revised Standard Version (NRSV) of the Bible directs our attention to the subjective qualities of faith. Other translations direct our attention outward. The Revised English Bible (REB), for example, speaks of the consequences of our faith: "Faith gives substance to our hopes" (11:1, REB). Faith substantiates what is unseen, as in the Creation God's word or command brought the material world into being (11:3). Such a translation highlights the rewards, the achievements, and the eventual outcomes that still lie ahead (11:6, 8, 13, 16, 20, 26, 32-34, 39-40). The paraphrasing in The Jerusalem Bible (JB) suggests a combination of the subjective and the objective qualities of faith: "Only faith can guarantee the blessings that we hope for, or prove the existence of the realities that at present remain unseen" (11:1, JB). A guarantee and proof suggests the surety felt within, but also points toward a realization of the state of affairs in the future.

Faith as assurance, conviction, and substance are illustrated in Hebrews 11:6b-38. As in the focus highlighted elsewhere in the Letter to the Hebrews, the examples of faith come from the early period in Jewish history, including Abraham, Moses, and the pre-monarchical period of the sojourn to the Promised Land. This focus directs our attention to the continuing journey into the future.

Acceptance

The treatment of the inward qualities and the outward consequences of faith is announced in the first verse of Hebrews 11. The author follows with the relationship established with God as a result of faith:

> By faith Abel offered to God a more acceptable sacrifice than Cain's. Through this he received approval as righteous, God himself giving approval to his gifts; he died, but through his faith he still speaks. By faith Enoch was taken so that he did not experience death; and "he was not found, because God had taken him." For it was attested before he was taken away that "he had pleased God." And without faith it is impossible to please God, for whoever would approach him must believe that he exists and that he rewards those who seek him.
>
> (Hebrews 11:4-6)

Being well-attested (11:5), being well-pleasing to God (11:5), and receiving approval as being right (11:4) are serious concerns. Faith can evoke rejection, alienation, hazards, persecution, and death (11:25, 27, 35-38; 12:2); but we are first reminded of an acceptance from God that is greater than human rejection.

Two examples of divine acceptance related to faith are cited. Abel's offering was acceptable because of faith (11:4). Faith can be understood in this setting as a trust in God's graciousness rather than a reliance upon our acceptability by what we have done or the person we think we are.

Enoch represents a dramatic kind of acceptance (11:5). The writer used the word *taken* and the reference to not seeing death as a graphic way of illustrating divine acceptance. To be taken or grasped by God dramatized that acceptance. Not seeing death was a suggestion that the death for humankind that ensues from sin was averted because Enoch was so acceptable.

These references to divine acceptance come before the rehearsal for the deeds of the faithful. Salvation is seen as a process moving from justification (or divine acceptance) to sanctification (or changes in character and hence in behavior). Often the reverse of this process has been thought to be the normative pattern in many religions. Christians can relapse into the same error. Prior to his conversion, Paul, for example, had thought works of righteousness that adhered to the Jewish law would gain divine acceptance for him. He discovered such was not the case. In his epistles he proclaimed that trust in God's graciousness prompted an inward sense of acceptance that, in turn, became the grounds out of which good deeds grew. People working earnestly, and perhaps feverishly, to do something that would gain them acceptance from God could not please God. Trust could. And God's acceptance has a way of creating changed behavior (Romans 5:1-5; Ephesians 2:8).

The writer of Hebrews was not as explicit as Paul about this sequence of divine acceptance from trust to good works (or the movement from justification to sanctification). This theology is detectable as we move from Hebrews 11:2, 4-6a, concerning divine acceptance from faith, to the righteous deeds of the faithful in Hebrews 11:7-40.

A survey of major figures from Noah through the early years of Israel's nationhood follows. The history, of course, cannot be complete in this sketch. As noted earlier, Abraham, Moses, and the judges are particularly prominent, all in keeping with this emphasis in other portions of the epistle. The connections will be drawn in order to explain the way the teaching is expanded.

Noah
(Hebrews 11:7)

The survey begins with Noah. He is held up as a model of faith because he trusted God's word concerning an impending flood and obeyed God's command to construct an ark. Although the enterprise made him a laughingstock among his peers, he persevered in that trust and obedience of faith. The flood vindicated him: his mockers stood condemned. His faith made him an heir of rightness. The important point was not that he was proved right and other people wrong, but that he lived a life attuned to the events in which God was acting.

Sometimes those who hear God's word find themselves at odds with those who believe the word from other sources. Estimates of our situation and their eventual outcome can vary drastically. Faith involves trusting in God's words, God's estimate, and the course of events God is working out. Taking that stance can place us in stark contrast to others who perceive the situation very differently. Listening to God's word and following that calling can make us "outsiders" and marginalize us. We can be "en route" a long time before we find a small portion of fulfillment.

Abraham and Sarah
(11:8-19)

Abraham and Sarah illustrate trust and obedience of persevering faith. Three events are noted. First there was the Promised Land. They were sojourners living in tents. They lived with a promise and not the realization of that promise. To their dying days, they were sojourners and aliens, even when they eventually took up residence in the land God had said would be theirs. When Sarah died, Abraham's neighbors told him to take a plot of ground for her burial. He insisted on paying for it because he said, "I am a stranger and an alien residing among you; give me property among you for a burying place, so that I may bury my dead. . . . I will give the price of the field . . ." (Genesis 23:4, 13).

Second, there was a son. Through faith in the promise, Abraham and his wife Sarah received the son of promise, Isaac. But a son did not make them parents of many nations. They had only tasted the first signs of that eventual fulfillment, just as establishing residence in the land of promise did not mean they had actually become people of that land.

Third, God asked Abraham to offer that son as a sacrifice, trusting God to raise up that son so that the longed-for promise of nationhood through their progeny could be fulfilled. Believing in that promise, Abraham took all the steps to fulfill the command. But the son was not taken when Abraham obeyed. Even then, the eventual promise of nations from their descendants had not been fulfilled (Genesis 22:1-19).

Whether in the case of the land, a son, or the sacrifice, Abraham and Sarah saw only glimmerings of that eventual fulfillment. Their faith, which was characterized by hope, sojourns, and patient waiting for a son, recalled the struggles associated with faith.

People who live with such a faith make themselves different from those around them. Any fulfillment of the promises of God they experience is a glimmering of the fuller substantiation of their trust in God. They do indeed become "strangers and exiles on the earth," still seeing that promise in the distance and greeting it from afar. They are truly "outsiders, en route," or "marginalized migrants."

The writer of Hebrews would agree with the writer of Ephesians. Christians are "no longer strangers and aliens" (Ephesians 2:19) in relation to God. God made that point concerning the acceptance of the faithful (Hebrews 11:2, 4-6). The writer of Hebrews made it very clear how Christians remain "strangers and exiles" in their relation to the world about them. They are comparable to those Jewish people in the wilderness sojourn, who were told again and again what they were to leave behind (5:11–6:12) and what they must press toward (4:9-11; 12:18-29; 13:12-14). They were en route—sojourners—and, in contrast to their neighbors, they were "outsiders"—strangers and exiles on the earth.

The references to Jacob and Joseph are brief (Hebrews 11:21-22) and illustrate further the forward look of Abraham and Sarah. They lived with the promise of God, with the eventual course of events that they saw as if it were already actualized. They were living in two worlds, in hope and in their immediate environment, just as the writer spoke of the present world as a shadow of that world of promise in Hebrews 9:6-10.

Moses
(11:23-28)

A sizable block of material is given to Moses. Although Moses was accepted by the very highest levels of Egyptian society as an Egyptian, Moses retained his Hebrew identity and "refused to be called a son of Pharaoh's daughter" (11:24). That identity could have given him many privileges and security, but he chose "rather to share ill-treatment with the people of God than to enjoy the fleeting pleasures of sin" (11:25). He was marginalized from those centers of power and privilege that were available to him because he identified with his own people.

His work of liberation with the people required a risky act (11:27). His deeds pointed toward an eventual fulfillment he himself was not to enjoy. He did not enter the Promised Land. Their deliverance at the Red Sea (11:29), and eventual entrance into the Promised Land came by faith, a faith exercised by Joshua and the harlot Rahab (11:30-31).

Further Sketches

Then follows a hurried sketch of others covering the period of Judges and the early monarchy:

> And what more should I say? For time would fail me to tell of Gideon, Barak, Samson, Jephthah, of David and Samuel and the prophets—who through faith conquered kingdoms, administered justice, obtained promises, shut the mouths of lions, quenched raging fire, escaped the edge of the sword, won strength out of weakness, became mighty in war, put foreign armies to flight. Women received their dead by resurrection.
> (Hebrews 11:32-35a)

This passage highlights the achievements. They call attention to the accomplishments of faith. We are clearly in the realm of the words of faith. These achievements are balanced with a recollection of suffering.

> Others were tortured, refusing to accept release, in order to obtain a better resurrection. Others suffered mocking and flogging, and even chains and imprisonment. They were stoned to death, they were sawn in two, they were killed by the sword; they went about in skins of sheep and goats, destitute, persecuted, tormented—of whom the world was not worthy. They wandered in deserts and mountains, and in caves and holes in the ground. (Hebrews 12:35b-38)

The emphasis on suffering is strong. It leads the author to come close to withdrawing what he said earlier—Abraham and Sarah "obtained the promise" (6:15). Now the emphasis in the context of suffering leads the writer to highlight how much still remained unfulfilled.

> Yet all these, though they were commended for their faith, did not receive what was promised, since God had provided something better so that they would not, apart from us, be made perfect. (Hebrews 11:39-40)

Faith Looks to Jesus

The impact of the passage is to bring before us a course of events in the grand drama of God's work, a long story of those with persevering faith who look beyond the present with hope and look to Jesus. In the earlier comparisons of Jesus with angels, Moses, Joshua, the priests, the old covenant and its laws, and the impressive sacrificial system, the author cited some of the weights and sins that cling so closely. In Hebrews 11 he told us about continuing our sojourn as he told us earlier to strive to enter the rest (3:1–5:10). In this context of the struggles and sufferings of the persevering faith, he tells us what Jesus did.

> *Instead of* the joy set before him, he endured the cross, despising the shame, and is seated at the right hand of the throne of God. (Hebrews 12:2, emphasis added and translation paraphrased)

The word the NRSV translates as "for" [in the phrase "for the joy that was set before him"] (*anti* in Greek) is most generally translated as "instead of" elsewhere. If we translate *anti* in the same way in this setting, rather than switch to "for," the example of Jesus would make more sense because of the choices that Jesus had, as well as what the readers of Hebrews were apparently facing (12:3–13:25).

Pilgrimage of the Faithful
(Hebrews 12:3–13:25)

In this section, we will examine Hebrews 12:3-17, 18-29, and 13:1-25 in that order. The interconnections between these subunits of Hebrews can be drawn in various ways.

One way is to organize the section that remains around the figures of Jesus as priest, royal person, and prophet. None of these figures are mentioned explicitly; however, the emphases that appear can be interpreted in light of these roles. The conversion of suffering into discipline that produces peace and righteousness (12:3-17) points to the priest who offers "grace to help in time of need" (4:16). The throne of God in Zion and the thorough triumph depicted in Hebrews 12:18-29 are best interpreted as a reference to a royal figure. The concrete imperatives that dominate Hebrews 13:1-25 are characteristic of a prophet.

Another way to see the movement of thought in the last section is to focus on Jesus who, "[instead] of the joy that was set before him endured the cross, disregarding its shame, and has taken his seat at the right hand of the throne of God" (12:2). The fact that Jesus "endured the cross, disregarding its shame" provides a model to interpret Hebrews 11:1–12:3.

This theme of enduring the cross and despising the shame led the writer to speak of converting suffering into discipline (Hebrews 12:3-17). The reference to the ensuing reign of Jesus with God on the throne set the stage for the references to the Awesome One in Hebrews 12:18-29, which then called for righteous living described in Hebrews 13:1-25.

Discipline and its Outcome
(Hebrews 12:3-17)

> Consider him who endured such hostility against himself from sinners, so that you may not grow weary or lose heart. In your struggle against sin you have not yet resisted to the point of shedding your blood. And you have forgotten the exhortation that addresses you as children—
>> "My child, do not regard lightly the discipline of the Lord,
>>> or lose heart when you are punished by him.
>> for the Lord disciplines those whom he loves,
>>> and chastises every child whom he accepts."
>
> Endure trials for the sake of discipline. (Hebrews 12:3-7a)

Given the model of the "pioneer and perfecter of our faith" who "[instead] of the joy that was set before him endured the cross, disregarding its shame" (12:2), the writer encouraged the believers to endure suffering as a discipline that comes from a divine Parent. The author assured them that God "disciplines us for our good" (12:10) and that they should therefore "be subject to" our gracious Parent (12:9).

While this concept suggests trust and faith, the writer did not encourage passivity. The readers were called to "lift . . . drooping hands and strengthen . . . weak knees, and make straight paths" (12:12-14). The experience of discipline "yields the peaceful fruit of righteousness to those who have been trained by it" (12:11) and yet they are to "pursue peace . . . and holiness" (12:14).

Another dual quality is noted. The writer was interested in Melchizedek, king of righteousness, who is king of Salem or peace. The combination of peace with justice or righteousness appeared earlier at other crucial points and in Hebrews' concluding benediction: The blessings of the "God of peace" brought with them an encouragement that readers be equipped with good to do God's will (righteousness), which was working in them (13:21), much as the covenant was to write the law of God on their hearts (8:10b-12).

An Awesome Meeting
(Hebrews 12:18-29)

The reference to Esau's greed that caused him to sell his birthright (12:16-17) led the writer to speak of the awesome God. If the God manifest on Sinai made Moses "tremble with fear" (12:21), the manifestation of God on Mount Zion was even more awesome. The splendor and grandeur of associations of angels, firstborn, God as judge, spirits of the righteous made perfect, and Jesus recalled the dangerous opportunity they could not miss (12:22-24).

One further capacity of this God is cited in Hebrews 12:25-29. The work of this God is thorough, removing what can be shaken and securing what cannot be shaken. The image of God is one of consuming fire (12:29). The writer who could speak of the merciful and faithful high priest did not hesitate speaking of this terrifying God, expressed elsewhere as a royal figure.

It should be observed how immediate this God is in this context. The readers were no longer urged to approach as if God were distant (4:16). The readers had already come to God (12:18, 22). The pilgrimage of the faithful brought them to a mighty God who will secure the right, a restatement of the peace with rightness we have seen in another picture of the destination of Christians (4:9-10; 7:1-2).

The Good Life "Outside the Camp" (Hebrews 13:1-25)

In the presence of this fearsome God, the writer spelled out in detail the righteousness that the disciplining should produce (13:1-25). The references up to this point in Hebrews have been rather general concerning the righteousness, justice, and holiness that ought to characterize those who live peaceably. Now the imperatives become specific. They include hospitality to strangers (13:4), modesty with money (13:5-6), support of leaders (13:7, 17), watching false teachers about food taboos (13:9), and prayer for the author (13:18-19).

One imperative deserves a separate mention:

> Therefore Jesus also suffered outside the city gate in order to sanctify the people by his own blood. Let us then go to him outside the camp, and bear the abuse he endured. For here we have no lasting city, but we are looking for the city that is to come. . . . Let us continually offer a sacrifice of praise to God.
>
> (Hebrews 13:12-15a)

The imagery is the Day of Atonement when the animals that bore the sins of the people were burned outside the camp (Leviticus 16). Since Jesus suffered outside the city gate, the author compared the death of Jesus with the role of the sacrificial animals. The death of Jesus bore away the sins of many. The important point is that the suffering outside the camp sanctified the people. The ignominious death on the garbage heap outside the gate on Golgotha (or the place of the skull) actually sanctified people.

This is a graphic expression of the model for Christians, who are outsiders. The writer urges readers to "go to him outside the camp and bear the abuse he endured. For here we have no lasting city." The calling is clear: Be "outsiders, en route," become "God's sanctifying action among people." Earlier the writer said that discipline can yield "the peaceful fruit of righteousness to those who have been trained by it" (12:11). Here suffering can sanctify others as we meet Jesus outside the camp.

WHAT IT MEANS

Sanctifying Abuses Outside the Gate

The closing observation suggests that Christians move outside the familiar modes of divine expressions and meet Christ in what some may see as "the place of the skull" or a city garbage heap of human society. We are warned that resistance to this enterprise will prompt abusive treatment. But the affirmation is clear. As Jesus sanctified the people through the abuse outside the camp, so too we can promote sanctity in those places, peoples, and cultures that are seen as the garbage heaps of human society. Many of us have fled those places because, when we became Christians, Christian spokespersons said we ought to leave those places and come into the camp. Recovering the sojourner identity now suggests we go out there and release the redemptive actions of God.

Many of these concerns and predictions may sound like exaggerations. They are not. Applications to two contemporary issues will reveal the abuses prompted by those who suggest we move "outside the gate" of our familiar encampment. Both illustrations have to do with the medium of God's word and work. The first is the Bible translation familiar to us; the second is our nation, the United States of America.

The history of the translation and revision of Scripture is an interesting one. At nearly every critical point, great controversy has surrounded each effort. When the original Aramaic, Hebrew, and Greek texts were translated into Latin at the end of the fourth century, Jerome's work was greeted by suspicion, hostility, and with the accusation that the Bible was "no longer divinely inspired." Monks continued to copy the manuscripts through the centuries, however, and it is understandable that mistakes in copying were bound to appear.

When John Wycliffe took those Latin manuscripts and produced the first complete Bible in English in 1388, his efforts resulted in official condemnation and personal disgrace and the burning of his carefully prepared work. Forty-five years after his death at the hands of those who believed the Bible should not be available to ordinary people to read, his ashes were exhumed and thrown into the Thames River so that English soil would no longer be contaminated. Further violent reaction followed other successive translations, even up to present times when the Revised Standard Version of the Bible appeared in 1952. The National Council of Churches of Christ in the USA, which holds the copyright, has several envelopes of ashes that were sent by angry church people who indicated that the biblical translation that is now normative for most of us "deserved to be burned." Some claimed it was "a Communist plot."

When the NCCC recommended in 1981 that a new English language lectionary (selected portions of the Bible intended for public worship) be developed, great furor developed in many congregations. The committee recognized that inaccuracies in earlier manuscripts and previous English language translations of the original texts have sometimes tended to exclude women from the inclusiveness of the entire biblical message. Sometimes the translations have limited God's nature to masculine qualities, failing to affirm that both women and men are "made in God's image." And sometimes, therefore, because of the interpretation of these texts, it has been assumed that Jesus' maleness was the crucial element in his coming as our divine/human Savior. The committee hoped that more inclusive language would affirm God's intention, as declared in the Scripture itself, that the entire human family is God's people.

The United Methodist Church participated in this process through the NCCC inclusive language lectionary committee. The Reverend Jeanne Audrey Powers, one of the denomination's participants in this exploration, received many letters and petitions from United Methodists about this matter. Some reflected the same kind of vindictiveness that marked the reception of previous efforts at enabling the Scripture's message to be communicated with faithfulness. Here are a few samples:

> You should be sent to Russia where you belong. Women don't even have any morals anymore. You should be taken out and horsewhipped.

> You are just on your own self-centered ego trips, because I don't believe you intend any benefit to humanity except to serve your own egoistic purposes.

> It might help you to know how America feels. The Bible is of divine writ by men designated by God to write exactly what He meant to say. My God doesn't make mistakes.

> I would hate to be in your shoes. Your punishment is sure! When you people come to the time you breathe your last breath, let me know how it feels!

The spiritual issue cited here in relation to Bible translations appears in our worship as well. An extraordinarily rich collection of resources became available toward the end of the last century. See, for example, *Word and Table: A Basic Pattern of Sunday Worship for United Methodists,* revised edition 1980 (Nashville: Abingdon, 1980).

Thus, those who promote the movements of God through truer versions of the Bible that are consistent with the basic thrust of the biblical message are facing heated opposition. Resistance comes from those who insist on God speaking in familiar, even if misleading and damaging, terms. The issue comes to this: will we remain in the camp or release new movements of God outside the camp?

The second medium of God's word and work we consider is this nation, the United States of America. The vast majority of our people have come to associate our nation with a unique status in the modern world. Our ideas for the good life are seen as a blessing for humankind. Our economic system carries hopes to meet everyone's basic human needs, and more. Our military has turned back the threat of evil forces. We have come to associate a divine calling and holy mission with this country.

According to Godfrey Hodgson in *America in Our Time*, we once saw ourselves united for this mission.

> There was a sense at the beginning of the 1960s that the businessman and the unskilled laborer, the writer and the housewife, Harvard University and the Strategic Air Command, International Business Machines and the labor movement, all had their parts to play in one harmonious political, intellectual, and economic system.[1]

He adds, "A dozen years later, that system was in ruins."[2] Hodgson draws upon an observation by an American historian for support of this conclusion. In 1970, Andrew Hacker wrote:

> America's history as a nation has reached its end. The American people will of course survive; and the majority will continue to live comfortably.... But the ties that make them a society will grow more tenuous with each passing year. There will be undercurrents of tension and turmoil, and the only remaining option will be to learn to live with these disorders....
>
> ... Abroad they will either make peace with a world they cannot master, or they will turn it into a battle ground for yet another century of war. Closer to home, however, Americans will learn to live with danger and discomfort, for this condition is the inevitable accompaniment of democracy in its declining years.[3]

People will rally around leaders who promise restoration of past glory so that we can drown Hacker's grim reading of our situation that pervades the deeper recesses of our consciousness. As a rapid succession of leaders fails to establish what we romantically see as our former greatness, such interpretations will evoke mounting hostility.

A comparable point in the history of ancient Israel is worth recalling. As unredressed evils in their society increased, the prophets changed their message. Their society was beyond repair; God would end Israel's nationhood. While some continued clamoring for minor changes and others sought restoration after the destruction of their nation, a few called their people to become a new kind of medium of blessing to humankind. They did not need their nation. They could be exiles without a homeland and yet be a light of hope in a darkened world.

As can be expected, these prophets evoked angry rejection. Jeremiah, for example, was mocked and imprisoned. As their predictions were fulfilled and some tasted the ministry they promised, these rejected words of the prophets found their way into the canon and blessed succeeding generations. Jesus was among them. He said, "Foxes have holes, and birds of the air have nests; but the Son of Man has nowhere to lay his head" (Matthew 8:20), adopting the identity of the exile and sojourner.

In the same way, we need voices today that call us to believe God can move creatively and redemptively through us without the protection, plenty, power, and prestige we have associated with this nation. No matter how tactfully we couch this bidding, it will inevitably prompt hostility as challenges to our eminence become more obvious. While we seek the lasting city that is to come, we will have as our companion one who sanctifies others through his suffering because he released the powers of an indestructible life. Praise be to this God! Thanks be to God for this holy calling! Amen.

Suggestions for Reflection

1. Share the models of faith (pp. 90–94) that are particularly important to you. If doing this as a group, you may wish to divide into small groups so that everyone has a chance to speak. Cite specific passages and relate them to concrete situations in your life.

2. Review again the basic outline of prayer (page 3) and respond to God, whether in adoration, confession, supplication, thanksgiving, or intercession.

3. Summarize the meaning that is suggested for Hebrews 13:1-25 in "The Good Life 'Outside the Camp.'" Do you agree with the applications drawn for the United States today?

4. Set aside time to use this session as an occasion to review what has happened to you and your ability to hear God's word through group and individual study and your confidence to interact with God in an open and honest way. If you have kept a journal during this study, summarize some observations of changes that have occurred in your growth. Again, the pattern of prayer will provide a clue for closure to this phase in your "pilgrimage of faith" and provide opportunities to articulate next steps, especially in your prayers of supplication.

Appendix

The Son, the Lord of Hosts

We have seen salvation for individuals highlighted in the new covenant in Chapter 6, "Sustenance En Route" (Hebrews 8:10-12). The saving work of God through Jesus Christ, however, is much more comprehensive. That broader scope of his work is depicted in the identity of Jesus Christ as a son and a royal figure. (References to a son, and not a daughter, come from the ancient practice of primogeniture, where the firstborn son received the heritage.) If we miss the way the early church understood those concepts, we will trivialize who Jesus is and what he will accomplish. We will examine the fuller identity of Jesus and his work in five passages, namely Hebrews 1:5a; 1:5b; 1:8-9; 1:13; 3:6. The violence at a few points should not turn us away from the more comprehensive deliverance from sin and evil that God promises in Jesus Christ.

Hebrews 1:5a

First, in Hebrews 1:5a, God says, "You are my Son; today I have begotten you." The passage comes from Psalm 2:7. A Jewish reader, or a Christian knowing the Hebrew Bible, very likely would have recalled the earthly references, which immediately follow:

> "Ask of me, and I will make the nations your heritage,
>   and the ends of the earth your possession.
> You shall break them with a rod of iron,
>   and dash them in pieces like a potter's vessel."
>
> Now therefore, O kings, be wise;
>   be warned, O rulers of the earth.
> Serve the Lord with fear,
>   with trembling kiss his feet,

> or he will be angry, and you will perish in the way;
> for his wrath is quickly kindled. (Psalm 2:8-12)

Hebrews 1:5b

Second, the quotation "I will be his Father, / and he will be my Son" could have just as easily recalled 2 Samuel 7, where the passage appeared. In that passage, King David consults the prophet Nathan regarding whether he should build a temple. After all, he lived in a house built of fine cedar; shouldn't the ark of the covenant be housed in something more than a "tent"? Nathan is given the following message from God:

> When your days are fulfilled and you lie down with your ancestors, I will raise up your offspring after you, who shall come forth from your body, and I will establish his kingdom. . . . I will be a father to him, and he shall be a son to me. . . . Your house and your kingdom shall be made sure forever before me; your throne shall be established forever. (2 Samuel 7:12, 14, 16)

Again, the reference to a son in this passage is associated with social and political transformations, even if it has religious overtones. God is concerned about establishing the people securely in the land and assuring the people that they will have one of their own reign over them, not an alien whose interests may overlook the needs of the people.

Hebrews 1:8-9

Third, we read a reference to the Son in association with a reigning figure:

> But of the Son he says,
> "Your throne, O God is forever and ever,
>   and the righteous scepter is the scepter of your
>   kingdom.
> You have loved righteousness and hated wickedness;
> therefore God, your God, has anointed you
>   with the oil of gladness beyond thy companions."
>   (Hebrews 1:8-9)

This quotation, which comes from Psalm 45:6-7, carried weighty political connotations. Immediately before this promise, which was used to claim that the reign of the Son will be both righteous and secure, the psalmist offered details of what is involved in such a reign:

> In your majesty ride on victoriously
>> for the cause of truth and to defend the right;
>> let your right hand teach you dread deeds.
>
> Your arrows are sharp
>> in the heart of the king's enemies;
>> the peoples fall under you. (Psalm 45:4-5)

Hebrews 1:13

A fourth passage appears in Hebrews 1:13. "Sit at my right hand, / until I make your enemies a footstool for your feet" (quoting from Psalm 110:1). Again, we turn to the psalm itself for the connotations and associations that could have been evoked when reference was made to one who "sits at [God's] right hand":

> The LORD is at your right hand;
>> he will shatter kings on the day of his wrath.
> He will execute judgment among the nations.
>> (Psalm 110:5-6a)

Hebrews 3:6

In the fifth passage, where a reference to a son is associated with royal considerations, we find the Son faithful over a house. The Son will receive the heritage after he has assisted in building the household.

In these five passages, the writer of Hebrews has given us a fuller understanding of the identity and efforts of Jesus Christ. While God promises us in Christ salvation for individuals, Hebrews has also brought before us Jesus Christ, the Son of God, as the Lord of Hosts over a host of lords (Isaiah 1:9; Jeremiah 6:6), and reigns with justice and mercy. We are therefore encouraged to look to Jesus as "the pioneer and perfecter of our faith" (Hebrews 12:2).

Aids for Further Study

Either in their church libraries, or those of their pastors, participants are likely to find several useful and accessible resources for further study. In *The Interpreter's One-Volume Commentary of the Bible* (Nashville: Abingdon Press, 1971); 895–915, will be found a brief introductory essay and helpful analysis of Hebrews by Warren A. Quanbeck. Other resources discussing the content, audience, and author can be found in the following:

Dinkler, Erich. "Hebrews, Letter to the," *The Interpreter's Dictionary of the Bible. Volume E–J.* Nashville: Abingdon Press, 1962; 571–575.

Bruce, F. F. "Hebrews, Letter to the," *The Interpreter's Dictionary of the Bible. Supplemental Volume.* Nashville, Abingdon Press, 1976; 394–395.

DeSilva, David A. "Hebrews, Letter to the," *The New Interpreter's Dictionary of the Bible, D-H, Vol. 2,* Nashville, TN: Abingdon, 2007; 779-86.

The content and message of Hebrews are discussed by two authors whose insights are reflected in this study:

Manson, William. *The Epistle to the Hebrews.* London: Hodder Stoughton, 1951.
This work highlights the missionary implications of the Epistle.

Filson, Floyd V. *"Yesterday": A Study of Hebrews in the Light of Chapter 13.* Naperville, Illinois: Alec R. Robinson, Inc., 1967.
This work summarizes the total book from key phrases found in Hebrews 13.

The following books can be consulted for authorship, general orientation, and problems in particular verses.

Bruce, F. F. *The Epistle to the Hebrews.* Grand Rapids, Michigan: William B. Eerdmans, 1965.
Bruce expands on the views authored by Manson, mentioned earlier.

Buchanan, George Wesley. *To the Hebrews: Translation, Comment, and Conclusions.* Garden City, New York: Doubleday & Co, 1972.
This offers the most thorough analyses among items listed here and explores the possible influences on the audience from thought and practices represented by the Dead Sea Scroll community at Qumran. The Appendix in this study has drawn heavily from Buchanan, pp. 38–51.

Jewett, Robert. *Letter to Pilgrims: A Commentary on the Epistle to the Hebrews.* New York: Pilgrim Press, 1981.
Applications to contemporary issues, based on careful analysis. Using parallels with Colossians, he argues for Epaphras as the author.

Montefiore, Hugh. *A Commentary on the Epistle to the Hebrews.* London: Adam & Charles Black, 1964.
A careful treatment, including an exploration into the possible relationship between First Corinthians by Paul and Hebrews, which Montefiore claims was written by Apollos.

Glossary

ABLUTION: A ceremonial washing practiced in many religions, including Judaism.

ANGELS: Messengers of God's word and implementers of divine intentions.

APOLLOS: A Jew from Alexandria, known for his able use of Scriptures and once a follower of John the Baptist. He was converted at Ephesus by Priscilla and Aquila and later worked in Corinth. He is regarded by some as the author of the Epistle to the Hebrews.

APOSTASY: A desertion or abandonment of one's belief.

APOSTATIZE: To desert or abandon one's beliefs.

APOSTLE: A title designating an early disciple who had seen the resurrected Jesus.

AQUILA: A tentmaker like Paul the apostle and the husband of Priscilla, a prominent woman in the early Christian church.

BARNABAS: A Levite from Cyprus associated with disciples at Jerusalem. Upon his conversion, his name was changed from Joseph to Barnabas, meaning "son of encouragement." He became Paul's traveling companion. He is regarded by some as the author of the Epistle to the Hebrews.

CANON: A list of writings considered to be normative for faith and practice.

COVENANT: An agreement establishing a bond between God and humankind, articulating promises or pledges from God and corresponding human responses.

CYPRIAN OF ANTIOCH: A Christian martyr who lived c. A.D. 300.

DAVAR: A term in biblical Hebrew language that can be translated as word or event, message or act, communication or occurrence.

ESSENES: A Jewish sect known as the "pious ones," leading a simple communal life, and contemporary with Jesus and the early church.

HEBREWS: Jewish converts to Christianity who spoke the Hebrew language or Aramaic, a Semitic language with many similarities with Hebrew. Hebrews were distinguished from Hellenists, Jewish converts who spoke Greek. Hebrews sought to retain more of the ancient Jewish practices in Christianity than the Hellenists who were exposed to Gentile cultures.

HOMILY: An oral interpretation of God's message, such as a sermon.

KING: A royal office instituted in ancient Israel after their occupation of Palestine and subsequently used as a symbol of capacities associated with God.

LAYING ON OF HANDS: A symbolic gesture communicating the Spirit and thus designating an assignment, conferring of office, or inducing health. In some cases, it was seen as transmitting human guilt to a sacrificial animal, as in the case of a scapegoat.

LEVITES: Ministers in the sanctuary, supposedly descending from Levi, including both Moses and Aaron, among others.

MELCHIZEDEK: According to Genesis 14:18, a king of Salem who was the priest of the Most High God. The name literally means, king of rightness, combining personal piety, social justice, and soundness in the cosmos. He is also mentioned in Psalm 110:4 as an eternal priest. References to Melchizedek appear in Hebrews in Chapter 7.

MOUNT SINAI: A mountain in the desert between Egypt and Palestine where Moses delivered the law to the ancient Israelites.

MOUNT ZION: A portion of Jerusalem taken by David from the Jebusites, later signifying God's holy hill at Jerusalem (Psalm 2:6), or the city itself (Isaiah 1:27), and typifying the heavenly city (Hebrews 12:22 and Revelation 14:1).

PAUL: A prominent apostle to the Gentiles and the author of a number of letters included in the biblical canon. Some regard Paul as the author of the Epistle to the Hebrews.

PRIESTS: Religious leaders in ancient Israel performing such functions as offering prayers and sacrifices, as well as writing histories and providing moral guidance in laws. A figure used to interpret the roles that Christ fulfills.

PRISCILLA: Sometimes referred to as Prisca, an early Christian convert, and wife of Aquila. Regarded by some as the author of the Epistle to the Hebrews.

PROPHET: One who is called to communicate between the divine and human worlds. Prophets are understood variously as those who reveal and proclaim God's will for moral and ethical life and proclaim both judgment and hope. Biblical prophets generally addressed the social and political circumstances of their own time. Christians look back to their words in the Bible as ways of understanding God's saving action through Jesus Christ.

PROSELYTE: A convert to a religious belief.

QUMRAN COMMUNITY: A community associated with the Dead Sea Scrolls, located above the northwest shores of the Dead Sea in the Judean hills. The ideas and practices of this community are thought by some to have influenced the readers of the Epistle to the Hebrews.

SHALOM: A word in the Hebrew language, sometimes appearing as Salem, meaning peace, wholeness, or soundness.

SHAMA: A word in biblical Hebrew language that can be translated as hearing and obeying, listening and acting in accordance with what is received.

SON OF MAN: A New Testament title for Christ (see Mark 14:62) that draws on Daniel 7:13 (RSV) that describes the Son of man as one who prevails over evil.

ZEDEK: A biblical Hebrew word usually translated as righteousness, but probably more appropriately as rightness since it includes personal piety, social justice, and wholeness in the total created order.

Notes

Chapter 1: The Living Word
and Community Renewal

1. Martin Buber, *I and Thou,* translated by Ronald Gregory Smith (Edinburgh: T. & T. Clark, 1937), 11.

Chapter 2: The Epistle of Paul the Apostle
to the Hebrews

1. The case for Barnabas has drawn on a summary offered by John A. T. Robinson in his book *Redating the New Testament* (Philadelphia: The Westminster Press, 1976), 217–219.

2. *Priscilla: Author of the Epistle to the Hebrews and Other Essays* (New York: Exposition Press, 1969), 110.

3. Hugh Montefiore, in *A Commentary on the Epistle to the Hebrews* (London: Adam and Charles Black, 1964), 9–31, provides a summary of a case for Apollos. See, too, Alexander C. Purdy, "Introduction" to the Epistle to the Hebrews in *The Interpreter's Bible* (New York: Abingdon Press, 1955), Volume II, 577–595, especially 581–583 and 590–591.

4. Walbert Bühlmann, "Mission in the 1980s: Two Viewpoints," *Occasional Bulletin of Missionary Research,* IV, 3 (July 1980), 98. See also W. Eugene March, *God's Tapestry: Reading the Bible in a World of Religious Diversity* (Louisville: Westminster John Knox Press, 2009), 20–21.

5. Orrin H. Pilkey and Wallace Kaufman, Jr., *The Beaches Are Moving* (Garden City, New York: Doubleday/Anchor, 1979), 219.

6. F. Thomas Trotter, "State of the Board," *1979 Yearbook,* edited by Martha Lawrence and Roy I. Sano (Nashville: Board of Higher Education and Ministry, 1979), 25–26.

7. In subsequent chapters, we will discuss the dangers of drifting away from following the pioneer of our salvation

(ch. 3), the destination (ch. 4), points of departure (ch. 5), sustenance along the way (ch. 6), and perseverance when we meet resistance (ch. 7).

Chapter 3: A Pioneer Worth Following

1. Marshall McLuhan, *Understanding Media: The Extensions of Man* (Cambridge: The MIT Press, 1964).

2. For Hebrews 1–2, see pp. 21–30; for Hebrews 3–6, see pp. 37–43; for Hebrews 7–10, see p. 79; for Hebrews 11–13, see pp. 94–95.

3. The author has said something similar in the opening verses. The Son bears more than a "family resemblance" to the divine Parent. "He is the reflection of God's glory and the exact imprint of God's very being. . . ." The divine glory is not only expressed, but the divine functions are executed as the Son upholds the world (1:3).

4. Two sequences of ideas are worth noting since they appear frequently and bear on the possible author.

• Concerning our behavior, the author *combines warnings with encouragement* in 2:1-5 and 2:14-18 (see pp. 27–30); 3:16–4:10 and 4:11-16 (see pp. 41–43); 6:4-6 and 6:9-20 (see pp. 61–63); and 10:26-31 and 10:23-39 (see pp. 76–80).

• Concerning our understanding of Jesus or God, the author combines an awesome portrayal with a reassuring picture in 1:5-29 and 2:10-18 (see pp. 26–29); 3:1–4:13 and 4:14–5:3 (see pp. 36–43); and 12:18-29 and 13:12-15a (see pp. 96–97).

The author's move toward encouragement from a gracious God lends support to those who claim Barnabas, "son of encouragement," wrote the Epistle.

5. This kingly quality that is central here, as elsewhere (1:5; 1:8; 3:6; 10:29), can be distinguished from other references to a Son where the emphasis lies (a) on telling forth God's word or expressing God and therefore the prophetic role (1:2); or (b) the priestly functions (7:3; 5:5-6). Though distinctions can be drawn between these various connotations of the word *son* or *Son,* in at least one instance, the roles overlap. In Hebrews 4:14, the high

priest is reigning in heaven, much as in other passages the Son is reigning. That is, priestly and kingly roles are combined in 4:14. See the Appendix, pp. 104–106.

6. "Break Thou the Bread of Life," words by Mary A. Lathbury, *The United Methodist Hymnal* (Nashville: The United Methodist Publishing House, 1989), 599, stanza 1.

Chapter 4: Pressing Toward Distant Destinations

1. See the Appendix, pp. 104–106, for the biblical basis for an elevated picture of the Son and the scope of the reign of the royal figure it suggests.

2. Quoted in *God's New Israel: Religious Interpretations of American Destiny* (Englewood Cliffs, New Jersey: Prentice-Hall, 1971), edited by Conrad Cherry, 64, and appearing originally in Irving L. Thomson, "Great Seal of the United States," *Encyclopedia Americana,* XLLL (1967), 362.

3. National Commission on the Causes and Prevention of Violence, *To Establish Justice, to Insure Domestic Tranquility* (New York: Award Books, 1969).

4. Ibid.

5. Ibid., 44–45.

6. Norman K. Gottwald, *The Tribes of Yahweh: A Sociology of the Religion of Liberated Israel 1250-1050 B.C.E.* (Maryknoll, New York: Orbis Books, 1979), 531. Mistranslations appear in such crucial passages as: Exodus 15:14; Joshua 2:9; 7:9; 9:3, 11; and Judges 5:23.

7. Adapted from a quotation in Frederick Turner's *Beyond Geography: The Western Spirit Against the Wilderness* (New York: Viking Press, 1980), vii.

Chapter 5: Points of Departure

1. Shusaku Endo, *Silence,* translated by William Johnston (Rutland, Vermont: The Charles E. Tuttle Company, 1969).

Chapter 6: Sustenance En Route

1. "The Sacrament of the Lord's Supper or Holy Communion," *The Methodist Hymnal* (Nashville: Board of Publication of The Methodist Church, 1964, 1966), 830 B.

2. This passage combines two figures that began the section where the royal figure, Melchizedek, king of Salem, is immediately identified with the priest of the most high God (7:1).

3. The same sequence of a warning and an encouragement has appeared in Hebrews 2:1-4 followed by 2:14-18; 3:16–4:10 followed by 4:11-16; and 6:4-8 followed by 6:9-20.

Chapter 7: The Unrelenting Sojourners

1. Godfrey Hodgson, *America in Our Time: From World War II to Nixon—What Happened and Why* (Garden City, New York: Doubleday and Company, Inc., 1976), 12.

2. Ibid.

3. Quoted in Hodgson, 13.

The Author

Roy I. Sano was born to immigrant parents from Japan in 1931. His father came across the Pacific, and then around the horn in South America, before he landed in Vera Cruz, Mexico. Later his father crossed the Rio Grande River near El Paso in 1907 and eventually settled in Brawley, California. His mother arrived from Japan in 1916.

Roy served in various pastoral ministries in California and New York City from 1951 until 1969. He became a chaplain and taught at Mills College in Oakland, California from 1969 until 1975. He was professor of theology at Pacific School of Religion in Berkeley, California, when he was elected a bishop in The United Methodist Church in 1984. He was assigned to the Denver and the Los Angeles Areas before his retirement in 2000.

Bishop Sano completed his undergraduate studies at UCLA and his basic theological training at Union Theological Seminary in 1957 in New York City. After receiving a master's degree from the Graduate Theological Union in 1968, he completed his Ph.D. in 1972 at Claremont Graduate University in Claremont, California.

In addition to this book on Hebrews, Dr. Sano published *From Every Nation Without Number: Racial and Ethnic Diversity in United Methodism* in 1982. He has also published a number of articles in journals and chapters in books.

Dr. Sano is married to Kathleen Thomas-Sano. He is the father of Topaz, Timothy, and Barton. Barton is married to Sharon. They have two children, Evan and Kira.

Roy enjoys working in the garden and walking in the woods, collecting rocks, and sauntering in museums of art.